GERMAN EXPRESSIONISM

In the same series

SEVEN EXPRESSIONIST PLAYS

Oscar Kokoschka *Murderer Hope of Womankind*
Franz Kafka *The Guardian of the Tomb*
Ernst Barlach *Squire Blue Boll*
Georg Kaiser *The Protagonist*
August Stramm *Awakening*
Alfred Brust *The Wolves*
Ivan Goll *Methusalem*

VISION AND AFTERMATH 4 Expressionist War Plays

Carl Hauptmann *War, A Te Deum*
Reinhard Goering *Naval Encounter*
Walter Hasenclever *Antigone*
Ernst Toller *Hinkemann*

FIVE PLAYS Georg Kaiser

From Morning to Midnight
The Burghers of Calais
The Coral
Gas I
Gas II

PLAYS VOLUME II Georg Kaiser

David and Goliath
The President
The Flight to Venice
One Day in October
The Raft of the Medusa

SCENES FROM THE HEROIC LIFE OF THE MIDDLE CLASSES

Carl Sternheim
The Bloomers
The Snob
Paul Schippel
1913
The Fossil

THE LULU PLAYS & OTHER SEX TRAGEDIES Frank Wedekind

Earth Spirit
Pandora's Box
Death and Devil
Castle Wetterstein

THE ERA OF GERMAN EXPRESSIONISM Edited by Paul Raabe

GERMAN EXPRESSIONISM

Series edited by J. M. Ritchie

SEVEN EXPRESSIONIST PLAYS

Kokoschka to Barlach

Translated from the German by
J. M. Ritchie and H. F. Garten

JOHN CALDER . LONDON
RIVERRUN PRESS   DALLAS

THE CALDER COLLECTION

Calder Publications is an imprint of

ONEWORLD CLASSICS LTD
London House
243-253 Lower Mortlake Road
Richmond
Surrey TW9 2LL
United Kingdom
www.oneworldclassics.com

Seven Expressionist Plays first published by Calder & Boyars Ltd in 1968
Reprinted by John Calder (Publishers) Ltd in 1980
This edition published by Calder Publications in 2010
Translations and Introduction © Calder Publications 1968, 1980, 2010

Mörder, Hoffnung der Frauen © Langen Müller, Germany; *Das Erwachen*
© Limes Verlag, Germany; *Der Gruftwächter* © S. Fischer Verlag, Germany;
Der Protagonist © Kiepenheuer & Witsch, Germany; *Methusalem* © L'Arche,
France; *Die Wölfe* © Cornelius Brust, Germany; *Der Blaue Boll* © Piper
Verlag, Germany.

Printed and bound in Great Britain by CPI Antony Rowe Eastbourne and
Chippenham.

ISBN (HARDBACK): 978-0-7145-4342-0
ISBN (PAPERBACK): 978-0-7145-4343-7

CONTENTS

INTRODUCTION

The task of making a new selection from the overwhelming mass of material produced by the Expressionist revolution is no easy one, for this was no small côterie of intellectual innovators or insignificant little avant-garde group, it was a tidal wave which for a time swept all before it. The Expressionists put their stamp on the cinema, painting, sculpture, music, architecture—but most of all they were active in the theatre. Here as elsewhere, the significant thing is the sheer mass of material. Very little of it is in any sense 'great' theatre, but buried among the forgotten rubbish is much of lasting value. Within Germany itself a process of rediscovery and reassessment is going on—many once famous plays, e.g. the sensational poetic, chaotic, ecstatic works of Sorge, Werfel and Johst prove almost unreadable and unplayable today while other lesser-known figures are growing considerably in stature. Of these Ernst Barlach the sculptor is the greatest.

Sokel has described Expressionist drama as a 'prelude to the absurd'. It must be admitted there is some justification for this but in some respects it might better be compared with the theatre of cruelty, with the rider that German Expressionist drama could on occasion be far more 'cruel' than anything even the fevered brain of Artaud ever imagined. Expressionist drama *is* 'cruel'. It is a theatre of gesture, noise, colour and movement, theatre which is not psychological but plastic and physical, theatre which is anarchic and dangerous, theatre in which violent images crush and hypnotise the sensibility of the spectator, theatre which is at times as devoid of speech as a silent film and at other times engulfs the listener in a storm-wave of words, theatre which is as deeply serious as it is grotesquely funny. All this was already attempted and in some cases achieved by the avant-garde experiments in Germany during the Twenties. But there is no need to describe Expressionist drama as a prelude to anything. It was a theatrical revolution in its own right, always deliberately unsettling, never nice or genteel and at all times prepared to exploit all the resources of the theatre.

Some of the artistic innovators of the time abandoned the spoken word entirely and arrived at a theatre of pure movement, light, colour and sound. Hugo Ball, for example who later became a leading Dadaist tried to create such a Theatre of the New Art. With the help of some painters e.g. Kandinsky, Klee and Marc and of some modern musicians he hoped to arrive at a new theatrical synthesis. Not unnaturally the painters tended to stress the colour, costume and stage design aspect of the theatre while the musicians strove for a theatre of pure sound; but the ideal was a synthesis in which the arts played an equal part as in Kandinsky's work *Der gelbe Klang* (The Yellow Chord). Unfortunately the Great War frustrated Ball's efforts to create a new theatre, but he did continue his experiments even during the war at the Galerie Dada in Zurich within the framework of the famous Dada soirées there at which Oskar Kokoschka's *Sphinx und Strohmann* was produced with stage design and special masks by Marcel Janco. Somehow between the immediate pre-war and the post-war years in Germany a vast amount of intensive experimentation sprang up in different centres. In addition to Hugo Ball and his Dadaists, there was the *Sturm-Bühne* arising from the group of artists and writers like August Stramm associated with Herwarth Walden and his avant-garde journal *Der Sturm;* there was Lothar Schreyer at the Hamburg *Kampfbühne;* and there were the abstract-constructivistic experiments carried out at the famous *Bauhaus* in Weimar by Oskar Schlemmer, Mohaly-Nagy and Schawinski. 'Theatre is the poetry of space' according to Artaud. Many years before him Oskar Schlemmer at the *Bauhaus* had taken this idea seriously and attempted to unite plastic and kinetic space forms with optic-acoustic formations.

However, it is with the literary drama which grew out of these extreme experiments that we are here concerned. It is incredible how many of the new theatrical possibilities worked out by experimental groups are already foreshadowed by Kokoschka's tiny *Gesamtkunstwerk Murderer Hope of Womankind* startlingly illustrated by the artist himself and later set to music by Hindemith. The cryptic title and the strangely mysterious and presumably sexual implications of its wording are a fair indication of the conflict within the play itself, namely a kind of primeval, demonic, Strindbergian battle of the sexes fought with enormous ferocity. The stage directions take up as much room as the actual dialogue, indicating that gesture and mime are as important as speech and are generally horrifying; *Old man with the iron: he rips open her dress and brands her. Woman screaming in terrible pain. Woman leaps at him with a knife and strikes a wound in his side. Man in convulsions, singing with a bleeding visible wound* etc. After a series of such horrors the play ends with an apocalyptic vision of the End of the World with Man victorious passing through all who stand in his path, slaughtering men and women like flies, while in the background there is a glow of red and from far, far away the crowing of a cock can be heard.

When this playlet appeared in print on the 14th July 1910 in the Berlin avant-garde journal *Der Sturm* whose circulation figures reputedly ran into tens of thousands, it is reported that its impact, combined with the shock of Kokoschka's illustrations for it, was so great that many cancelled their subscriptions. So Kokoschka's play immediately became the focal point of discussion for all the avant-garde groups of the time of which as has been seen there were many. This does not mean that the German theatres immediately welcomed this play with open arms, nevertheless *Murderer Hope of Womankind* (and its grotesque counterpart *Sphinx and Strawman*, the Wedekind-inspired 'Comedy for Automata') do mark the beginning of the new wave for Germany. Kokoschka's play is a violent reaction against the illusion of reality on the stage—instead it is clearly based on visionary explosions. One result of this was the extremely condensed form which was to set the pattern for so much of the Expressionist drama to follow; with the later adherents of the *Sturm* circle e.g. Stramm this was to develop into the condensed language characterised by the name Telegram Style. Instead of the old Naturalist style (called in German *Sekundenstil*, namely the attempt to capture the whole of reality as it happens second by second), we find now the elimination of all realistic detail, (time, place, profession etc.) and the focusing on essentials to the exclusion of all else. This is done by placing the action in an unspecified, Dionysian Classical Antiquity with no attempt whatsoever at capturing naturalistic milieu. In place of the detailed recording of external features to indicate character we find here only *Man, Woman— Night Sky, Tower*. Similarly the colours are deliberately 'unnatural' like the primary colours of Frank Marc's animals—blue armour, white face, yellow hair, red dress etc. while the gestures and general behaviour are 'convulsive' and more bestial than human—the Woman for example 'creeps round the cage like a panther' 'clings

9

high up in the air like a monkey'—and then 'writhes on the steps like a dying animal, her thighs and muscles convulsed'. Expressionist drama was often later to be derided as *Schreidrama* i.e. 'screamplay' and this element too is clearly very much in evidence in Kokoschka. The Man's 'savage' followers are heard first 'crying out in a slow crescendo'—the First Girl utters a piercing scream, the Woman cries out in terrible pain and later as she feels her end is near releases 'highest tension . . . in a slowly diminishing scream' while men and women fleeing from Man 'run into his way, screaming'. It is easy to laugh at so much screaming, especially in later abuses of the *Schreidrama*, but this too is a natural consequence of the Expressionist avoidance of natural everyday existence in favour of the Absolute, life at the point of 'highest tension'. This kind of play is never intended as a portrayal of normal life in normal speech, it is the symbolic or rather plastic, colourful and explosive vision of an existential situation. Kokoschka's little play which seems an incoherent picture of ritual blood-lust is a return to myth expressed through quasi-biblical imagery and rhythmical chanting of poetical language which constantly soars higher and higher into song. Yet this elevated language is never allowed to end in the merely 'poetic' or aesthetically pleasing—there are enough screams and horrors to stop this—Kokoschka avoids the sublime by the use of the 'grotesque'. This was also to become one of the hall-marks of the later Expressionist drama. Tragedy is not possible any longer, only a balancing act between the tragic and the comic.

It could be argued that such tragi-comic grotesque treatment of the Freudian sex-war had already been demonstrated theatrically by Strindberg who certainly produced the greater literary works, but it was Kokoschka who was first to be completely consistent in removing all the associative links and eliminating all attempts at neat summing-up. He leaves nothing but the existential war of the sexes as a cosmic experience. It is no mere conjecture but established fact that Kokoschka knew and built on the plays of Strindberg which he had seen in his native Vienna. There he also became acquainted with the works of Freud. In addition attention has recently been drawn to the once famous book by Otto Weininger, namely *Sex and Character* which appeared in Vienna in 1903 only four months before the suicide of its author. This work goes a long way towards explaining the cryptic title to Kokoschka's play.

Sex and the battle of the sexes is an important element in the world of Kokoschka as it had been in that of Strindberg but at least as far as German drama is concerned this battle had already been fought out by Frank Wedekind the cabaret artist and singer of crude street ballads whose plays from *Spring's Awakening* on deal with this basic theme, in some part at least even with a violence equal to Kokoschka's own; in *The Earth Spirit*, for example, or *Pandora's Box* which finishes with Lulu the eternal woman being disembowelled by Jack the Ripper before the very eyes of her Lesbian friend. Sex in fact was to become one of the main themes of Expressionism in the narrative as well as the dramatic forms as has been demonstrated by a recent anthology of Expressionist prose called *Ego und Eros* which the compiler himself describes as a wild book . . . 'wading up to the elbows in blood and up to the waist in women.' But more important than sex and the deliberately shocking treatment of its more lurid aspects is the basic situation of total conflict and rebellion, in many cases not merely of man against woman but son against father. Yet even this characteristic battle of the generations often took extreme sexual forms e.g. in the much quoted example of Arnolt Bronnen's *Patricide* in which a high-school boy has sexual intercourse with his mother on stage and mortally stabs his father. As Sokel says: 'this is not just Tennessee Williams Naturalism, not just a dramatisation of the Freudian Oedipus complex: it is the Freudian view of the artist—he has sublimated his misery into a dream and projected this dream onto the stage. With this, the keynote of Expressionism is struck: *subjectivism.* Dream as literature.'

What Kokoschka and after him so many Expressionist dramatists give then is no naturalistic illusion of real life but a Strindbergian 'Dream Play' in which all the resources of the modern stage (particularly the spotlight) conjure significant optical illusions, colours, choreographic groupings and gestures out of the surrounding darkness. Drama now relies more on expressive pantomime than on words. Meaning, however, is not absent—far from it. It is simply no longer spoken, it is enacted. *Murderer Hope of Womankind* for example is not an 'absurd' play despite its appearance of chaos, it is an early example of what was to become in later Expressionists the *Erläuterungsdrama*, the drama of purification. The playlet enacts a myth of the purification of man who dies to be reborn—to walk through the world as The New Man. The message for mankind is the need for the 'regeneration of man'.

As has been seen from the example of Kokoschka condensation and compression was to become an important element on the way to paring down to the quintessential. The result was an economy in form going beyond even the extreme simplicity of the Greek classical drama invoked by the Pindaric utterance and classical setting of Kokoschka's play. Instead of the social criticism of the naturalist theatre the new play becomes a cry of despair at the state of the world, a quest for meaning in apparent chaos, a scream. Sometimes the result is incoherence, more often however the scream is compressed into cold clear form. The process of reduction, condensation and concentration was extreme—everything was reduced to the bare minimum: language especially was pared down to the language of the telegram, hence the famous staccato, hard, brutal, machine-gun effect of the Expressionist Telegram Style. Hector Maclean has described this in his recent study of Expressionism. Language it was felt must regain its dynamic quality, it must be delivered from its organisation into familiar structures and associations, from the certainty that one word automatically follows another in speech and writing—language must be delivered from the enslavement of syntax:

> Language controlled by syntax was regarded as rational language and the language of reason presupposes a world of repose and rigidity, which is exactly what Marinetti's *Technical Manifesto* was intent on destroying. Marinetti's opposition was directed basically against normal syntax as reflecting compartmentalised thinking. He advocates the removal of all defining and connecting elements. Conjunctions, adjectives and adverbs disappear, and together with them punctuation; the verb remains in the infinitive so that it can adapt elastically to the noun. The *naked* nouns themselves thus retain and enhance their essential character, and are linked directly by association and analogy, not by any logical train of thought.

In their most extreme form these requirements are scarcely practicable, but Marinetti's influence was clearly felt among members of the *Sturm* group of writers led by August Stramm who succeeds where others failed in producing language with the explosive power of the clenched fist, poems and plays intended to be a fever expressed in cold, clear language—a vision.

The Play *Erwachen* (*Awakening*) appeared as number 5 of the *Sturm* book series in Nov./Dec. 1915. Stramm had already experimented with lyrical drama (*Sancta Susanna* and *Haidebraut*) and naturalistic milieu drama (*Rudimentär*) but this was for him a completely new style though it has been maliciously whispered that as a high Post Office Official he was marked out by fate and profession to be the real inaugurator of the 'Telegram Style'. *Awakening* has the tempo of a silent film with all the miming, exaggerated gestures, long stares and silences one associates with this particular art-form. Sex does not play the main part in this play though the situation in which the Man and Woman are discovered is presumably an extracted essence of countless similar theatrical scenes with lovers surprised in a hotel bedroom. There is still something of the violence of Kokoschka's play in Stramm's *Awakening* with its dark threats and unexpected screams, money-lust, murder (the hotel-keeper) and sudden death (the absent husband) all compressed into one short sequence. As in the Kokoschka play the play is mainly a confrontation between Man and Woman who are singled out against a background of anonymous rabble and as in Kokoschka the Man is a kind of Nietzschean Superman, beyond good and evil, who survives at the end to point into the new dawn. Once again this is no mere demonstration of the 'absurd' despite the He, She and It protagonists and the characteristic vision of the city tottering on the brink of destruction, about to be engulfed in flames only to be saved by water when the dam gates are opened. The play has a meaning—but it is one best expressed through its own concrete imagery. The breaking down of the bedroom wall opens the way to a glimpse of something cosmic, something high above the world of a hotel bedroom. *He* sees this in the star while *She* remains tied to bourgeois concepts of marital fidelity and love of her children. But though *She* is incapable of the higher flight and accepts the abuse of the mob as just, her sister (*It*) has eyes to see. The title then refers to the sister's *awakening* by *Him* to full womanhood in the same way perhaps as Kokoschka's woman is awakened to an awareness of full womanhood. She sees in him the genius, the super-man, the master-builder who has created the city out of his brain. She is awakened from an *It* to a *She*. The mob meanwhile feels threatened by the incursion of genius into their world and tries to drag him down (Kokoschka's play too starts with men trying to pull Man's horse to the ground) but the master-mind marches through them and through the general destruction as he does at the end of Kokoschka's play. Kokoschka's play finishes with the cock crowing the dawn of a New Day; in Stramm it is the Christian image of the star which announces the birth of the New Man.

Between the two extremes of Kokoschka's rhapsodic singing style and Stramm's cold, hard, Telegram Style a wide range of variations was possible. Kafka's fragment *The Guardian of the Tomb* demonstrates his characteristic variety which has recently been described as a kind of classical Expressionism. Kafka may also be dealing with the Absolute in this nightmare vision of a castle on the borderline between 'the human sphere and the other', but he uses no formal or grammatical excesses. The whole grotesque situation is expressed in an apparently ice-cold style. Here again as in Kokoschka or Stramm there is little or no plot and almost no exposition or psychological motivation. The play consists essentially in the simple confrontation between the prince and the watchman and proceeds as a Socratic dialogue, a question-and-answer puzzle, which however, despite the appearance of calm and reasoned logic only succeeds in demonstrating the difficulty of arriving at ultimate truth. Once again as in Stramm's play we are locked in a timeless room in an unnamed country in an unknown age. But in this play too perspectives are opened up into cosmic reaches. Time seems suspended in an eternal recurrence of grotesque horror. How long have these nightmare visions, which, in typical Kafka fashion, we are told are no dreams, been going on? Every night the same battle is fought. Even here the sexual imagery is not lacking though it is more peripheral, as the conflict between the Prince and the Princess is not developed: after the exhausting battle between the 'bed-bug' and the Duke, sometimes when the Guardian is lying exhausted on the ground, 'a soft being, moist and hairy to the touch, comes to me . . . . She feels me in various places, puts her hand in my beard, lets her whole body glide over my neck under my chin . . ." And here too as in *Awakening* there is the 'eye' that sees through the confusion of external detail right to the heart of the matter: 'You see in the first hour the eternally obvious as clearly as if you've been seeing it for a hundred years.' But is it really possible to see so clearly, to have such positive knowledge? The whole play suggests not—and in fact is filled with inexplicable gestures and unexpected actions. The Guardian, for example, suddenly crouches behind the divan gesticulating wildly with his arms, or collapses with a little scream or raises his hand and strokes the prince's cheek. Little wonder that far from suggesting light and sanity Kafka's play, like Kokoschka's, shows little islands of light picked out of the threatening darkness by a momentary spotlight, and indeed the last words of this play which remained a fragment like so much of Kafka's work are those of the Princess: 'But I know it is getting blacker and blacker, this time it is an autumn sad beyond all measure.'

But Kafka is not remembered today for his excursion into the world of the theatre though he was not entirely unconnected with it. It is the sobriety of his prose tales which made him famous throughout the world. Nevertheless his cool, grotesque style is one which is also found in other Expressionist dramatists, especially Kaiser and Sternheim, and it is they who have proved the most enduring of the great mass of dramatists who appeared on the scene in Germany in the Twenties. Georg Kaiser is perhaps the better known of these two exponents of the cold hard style, in which to use his own words: 'violent emotion is met with cool speech—the molten metal must arrive as rigid form.' This combination of violent extremes expressed in calm logical language is certainly the one aimed at in his little play *The Protagonist* written in 1920 and first performed in Breslau in 1922. It was later set to music by Kurt Weill who collaborated with Kaiser on two or three plays before his more famous work with Brecht. Hugo Garten has described the main theme of this little play as—'the confusion of reality and illusion—with a Pirandellian touch'. The play as he sees it revolves round the intrusion of the real world upon the world of the imagination, or 'vice versa, the supremacy of the 'mind' over material facts, a definition which might also apply to Kafka's *Guardian of the Tomb*. In addition, however, one should perhaps mention the unusual brother-sister relationship with the suggestion of vampirism that other critics have noticed. Here once again the characters are nameless and the action takes place in a bare shabby room grey with dust. Though the setting is given as Shakespeare's

England no time is wasted on historical accuracy or atmosphere. The protagonist is the supreme Expressionist artist possessed of a fever, a madness, a 'passion for transformation through the whole gamut from emperor to assassin'. The play is interesting for the image of the actor it presents. It is true the protagonist loses himself in his rôle, but what the actors perform is not any piece of naturalistic dialogue, but plays without words in which gesture, mime, improvisation and music are the important ingredients. Significantly too the distance between tragedy and comedy is reduced, the one becoming merely a reversal of the other. When the spicy play of sex and seduction no longer meets His Grace's requirements, the protagonist does not produce a serious play as requested, but exactly the same play in a different key: transposed to tragedy. 'For as every jest can be taken in earnest, we are not going to act a new play but simply transform our comedy into tragedy.' The play is then mimed out in this way like a silent film with 'crazed' behaviour, passionate embraces, unrestrained caresses, frenzy etc. until it ends in confusion and the actors and musicians are incapable of continuing. The protagonist himself, however, does not break off until, confronted by his sister and her secret lover, he *sees* the lie in her eyes where till then there had been only truth and the play ends in living horror with his dagger in her throat and the protagonist now capable of playing his 'best part, where there is no longer any distinction between real and feigned madness'. From first to last the play could be taken as a demonstration of alienation brought on by the projection of the artist into an imagined other life.

Bertold Brecht has some similarities with Kaiser and on occasion also turned to English sources. In *Mann ist Mann* for instance he sets a play within a play where the actors step in and out of their parts, but it has not been possible because of copyright difficulties to include any Brecht in this volume. Brecht often employed the zany surrealist dialogue reminiscent of the Marx brothers, but this was by no means unusual in the German theatre and was extensively exploited by the man whom Brecht himself described as 'The Expressionist Courteline'—Ivan Goll. Goll's translators in America, Clinton J. Atkinson and Arthur Wensinger have recorded recently the impact of Goll's major piece *Methusalem* (produced in Berlin in 1922 with direction by William Dieterle and décor by Georg

Grosz) which they characterise as an 'amazingly prescient work with entire scenes that reappear nearly verbatim in the much later work of Ionesco (particularly in the Bald Soprano).' It is perhaps more through his association with the French Surrealists that Goll is known today, but his background was in a sense typical of the whole Expressionist generation: 'by fate a Jew, born by chance a Frenchman, made by the whim of a rubber stamp, a German'. His work was dispersed over several languages and long forgotten by all but the discerning few. Yet as far as the theatre is concerned at least he was certainly much in advance of his time, especially in theory. His *Methusalem* follows in the tradition of Alfred Jarry's *Ubu Roi* and Apollinaire's *Les Mamelles de Tirésias* but the preface which he gives to this play shows that his aim was that of the German Expressionists, namely to 'strip away surface reality to reveal the Truth of Being'. Clearly Goll, like Brecht and most of the early Expressionists, was much involved with the contemporary discussions of the film medium and the futuristic techniques of *montage*, all of which he exploited. And it is not surprising to discover that he too, like Kokoschka, Kaiser and Brecht was associated with the musical theatre; he saw another work *Der Neue Orpheus* performed together with the opera *Royal Palace* in the State Opera House in Berlin in 1928 both set to music by Kurt Weill. Goll's play *Methusalem* is entitled a 'satirical drama'. The décor was by Georg Grosz who was already famous for his fierce attacks on the German bourgeois and this seems on the surface to be the aim of Goll's play. Yet the biblical title, reminiscent of another Kokoschka play (*Job*), is a reminder that this particular scourge of mankind has been in existence since the beginning of time and will go on indestructibly for ever. The dialogue employed is incredibly banal, the clichés rain unceasingly. Film sequences showing the inner workings of the bourgeois mind ridicule the fusion of the erotic with the materialistic, the exploitation of culture, the combination of the militaristic and patriotic with commercial interests. Humour in the modern world is debased into the product of a mechanical device, a Joke Box. The artificial or stuffed animals in the room come 'out of their unnatural positions' to move freely about the room, and celebrate a kind of *Animal Farm* revolution. Always it is the skilful use of lighting which 'brings out hitherto unnoticed objects—change of lighting takes

the place of change of scene.' The walls and windows, the very
pictures on the wall can come to life as they do in the scene in
which the lyrical maiden is contrasted with the typical dried-up
maiden aunt. Modern man is represented by Felix the counting
machine from the stock-market who metallically recites the world
news items of the day, none of which have any effect on Methusalem
whatsoever until he hears that his own personal interests are
endangered by a strike in his shoe factory. The strikers who appear
led by daughter Ida's student lover are quickly put down by six
armed policemen who spring from the safe. Always Methusalem
himself remains totally unaffected except when defending his own
interests. This he does very well.

The most striking scene is Ida's rendezvous which shows not
only a stage divided into two by split lighting, but a character
divided into three—the student appears played by three identical
masked players representing his Ego, his Superego and his Id.
Masks are also worn at the Methusalem's tea-party this time
representing Greed, Envy and Curiosity. Ida's Confession followed
by the Duel Scene are parodies of their typical equivalents in
countless middle-class tragedies—here with startling interruptions
by film sequences. In the duel itself the student is shot and his soul
floats upwards in the shape of an overcoat—but the departure of a
soul does not mean physical death and the student lives on, just as
Methusalem lives on, even after he has been shot by the student
while haranguing the revolutionary mob. While the student and
Ida sink into bourgeois mediocrity Methusalem appears again still
mouthing his platitudes and clichés.

Is all this intended to have any socio-political significance? Is the
animal revolution a parody of the human revolt or vice versa? Is
the attack on the bourgecis really so violent after all? One senses
that Goll like Sternheim and so many of the Expressionist contem-
poraries who launched their massive onslaughts on the philistine
secretly admired the anti-artistic, anti-intellectual nonchalance and
resilience of the bourgeois. In fact the image that probably remains
in the memory is not one of a shattered enemy but of Methusalem
contentedly farting in the face of the audience.

It seems a long way from the hectic metropolis of Goll's bourge-
oisie with its revolutionaries and human stock-market computers
to the brooding atmosphere of a primitive existence lived close to

nature portrayed by Alfred Brust's *The Wolves* (1922) but in fact the Expressionists, as has been seen, were attracted by the primitivism of the beast as much as by the cold objectivity of the machine. Brust's little play (from a set of three one-acters round the figure of Tolkening) is apparently perfectly normal in language and dramatic form. But the theme of the rather saintly country pastor with a completely demonic country wife is one of extreme violence. The play becomes an open conflict between the spirit and the flesh, a massive assault on life-denying Christianity and a demonstration by the woman of a longing for fulfilment in LIFE which goes far beyond the bounds of normal society. The play closes with a nightmare vision of the demonic woman who has cried: 'Oh, to be raped to death by a wolf' heading for her bedroom with her great red beast. Horrible noises are then heard and her naked body is then found on the bed with the throat ripped open.

But despite first appearances, this play is no naturalistic drama of domestic interior in lonely East Prussia. From the start the tempo is very slow and brooding. Tolkening is haunted by dreams. His newly arrived friend Dr. Joy is not the stock 'rescuer from afar' of the Naturalist drama but the Expressionist who pierces through surface reality to the heart of the matter and knows 'there is more going on than the eye can see'. Like the castle in Kafka's play this house with its light shining out into the surrounding darkness is on the borderland. The people of the village look up to the light, but behind the village stand the dark forests that stretch right through to Russia, even as far as Siberia: 'you can feel the great heart of Asia pulsing in your veins'. In the same way that the vast primeval forests are let into this one room, so too Dr. Joy makes us aware of the vastness of Time. It is he who develops the theory of the battle of the sexes that has been going on since the beginning of time, though Anita seems to have arrived at similar conclusions for herself. But in the end what really happens? Is it not all in the mind, a nightmare of the sex-starved Agatha exhausted by long travel, unusual surroundings and the threatening roar of the ice breaking which punctuates her dreams?

Critics were very quick to see the similarities between the work of Brust and that of the sculptor and wood carver Ernst Barlach. Here we are concerned with the sixth of his dramas *Squire Blue Boll* published in 1926. If Expressionist drama started with the artist

Oskar Kokoschka we find in Barlach too the same combination of talents so characteristic of the generation. Like Brust, Barlach appears to be giving an accurate description of small town life in this lonely part of Germany but like him he is far removed from any naturalistic intention of portraying social or economic conditions or advocating any kind of reform, despite his plot which revolves round poisoning, potential suicide, sudden death and sex. In fact his play is a deliberate reaction against the Naturalist theory that man is determined by milieu, race, class or any conditioning factor. Boll appears first as fixed in his place in society. 'How can Boll the landed gentleman help being Boll the landed gentleman? He is unasked, simply not asked whether he wanted to become Boll the landed gentleman or not.' He has been forced into a certain rôle in society which till now he has played well, enjoying the physical pleasures of his position to the full. Squire Boll is called blue because of the blood pressure and attacks of dizziness brought on by his excesses. He is the glutton and lecher his position has made him. But man is neither a machine nor a mere animal predestined to travel along certain paths. He is free to chose his own path. The path chosen by Boll is here presented in the form introduced by Strindberg, the *Stationendrama*. Instead of a well made play in five acts what we have here is a kind of mystery play in the epic form of seven stations or tableaux—showing the various stages on the path to Boll's 'becoming'. The theme of the play has been described by one critic as the 'excarnation of the self'. i.e. the freeing of the self from the embrace of the flesh and characteristically for an Expressionist play this is shown not in abstract terms but in the very concrete, plastic terms of the changing life of a fat man. The flesh is physically present on the stage. Put another way this makes the play revolve round the fundamental Expressionist theme of *Erneuerung des Menschen*, the regeneration of man, in this case by the birth of the New Man inside Boll. Always there are concrete images to express the abstract meaning. As in Kokoschka's little play the scene of the action is a tower (the scene too of Hofmannsthal's play of this time—*Der Turm*). It is the tower which by its hazy perspective at the beginning of the play suggests that there might be more behind things than meets the eye, that life doesn't always go according to plan, that everything is liable to unexpected change etc. At first Boll towers up himself arrogantly, but the episode in the room halfway up the tower undermines his self confidence. The confrontation in this room with the 'witch' Greta who is also obsessed with the problem of the flesh marks the parting of the ways for Squire Boll. He can either plunge down from the tower in quick suicidal change of direction or he can go upward to a new life. It is the latter choice which is eventually his, helped towards his final decision in one way or the other by all the characters of the play who are all involved in this process of change. Yet while this play by Barlach is clearly in the tradition of the play of ideas (*Ideendrama*) and the intellectual content is often rather dense, nevertheless the message is expressed not in language of sustained pathos, but in an awkward, earthy groping style which also seems to be in a state of becoming. Characteristically too the play is full of strikingly grotesque characters, incidents and situations which also avoid the dangers of excessive elevation of tone. Apart from the occasional blueness of Squire Boll's face there is the devil of a hindquarter which goes bounding round the town, a gentleman who may or may not be the Lord God himself and a demon-woman Doris who may be the devil's companion. Always the ambivalence is maintained—is the Gentleman really a force for Good who brings about Boll's reincarnation? He seems to drive Otto to death and Boll to the brink of suicide. Doris the demon-woman on the other hand seems to become a kind of Earth Mother who can take all the sins of the world upon herself, thereby purifying Greta the Witch. There is much in this play to remind one of Brecht. Apart from this curious alienation of character and incident, the drinking bout with Otto, the Squire and drunkard points to Brecht's later *Puntila* while the idea of God walking through the world points forward to the gods in *The Good Person of Szechwan*. But the play is not Brechtian—its striking feature is still that fundamental to all Expressionist drama, namely the *vision*. Even in the normal life of simple people in a small town in Germany the real world of values behind the world of appearances can suddenly be revealed. Eyes are opened to *see*! Greta who has been desperate to poison her own children to free their souls from the flesh suddenly sees their flesh being scorched off them in the Devil's Kitchen. Boll himself looks at the wooden apostle in the church and *sees*! From the description this wooden figure might have been carved by Barlach the artist and sculptor himself so 'expressive' is it, but

Barlach was not only a great sculptor, he was also a great literary artist. The Expressionist movement from Kokoschka on was characterised as has been seen by constant cross-fertilisation among the arts from painting and sculpture to music and mime but Barlach was perhaps the only one of the artists to create major works in the literary as well as the artistic field. His plays and especially *Squire Blue Boll* are among the most significant achievements of modern German drama.

Hull, July 1966   J. M. Ritchie

Recommended Reading

H. F. Garten: *Modern German Drama* (London, 1959)

Walter Gropius ed.: *The Theatre of the Bauhaus*
(Wesleyan University Press, 1961)

M. Hamburger & C. Middleton eds.:
Modern German Poetry 1910-1960 (London, 1963)

Claude Hill & Ralph Ley: *The Drama of German Expressionism*
A German-English Bibliography
(University of North Carolina Press, 1960)

Egbert Krispyn: *Style and Society in German literary Expressionism*
(University of Florida, 1964)

Hector Maclean: Expressionism in *Periods in German Literature*
ed. J. M. Ritchie (London, 1966)

Paul Raabe: *Expressionism* in preparation for late 1968 (Calder and Boyars)

J. M. Ritchie: German Theatre between the Wars and the Genteel
Tradition, *Modern Drama*, Feb. 1965
The Expressionist Revival, *Seminar*, Spring, 1966

J. M. Ritchie (ed.): *Vision and Aftermath*, four Expressionist War plays (Calder and Boyars, 1968)

R. H. Samuel & R. Hinton Thomas:
Expressionism in German Life, Literature and The Theatre, 1910-1924 (Cambridge, 1939)

Walter H. Sokel: *The Writer in Extremis: Expressionism in 20th Century German Literature*
(Stanford, California, 1959)
An Anthology of German Expressionist Drama
a prelude to the absurd (Doubleday Anchor, A365)

August Strindberg: *Eight Expressionist Plays*
(Bantam Classics, QC 261)

MURDERER HOPE OF WOMANKIND

1907

by Oskar Kokoschka

Translated by J. M. Ritchie

PERSONS

MAN
WOMAN
WARRIORS
MAIDENS

The action takes place in antiquity.
Night-sky.
Tower with great grid-iron door.
Torchlight.
Ground rising to the tower.

THE MAN
white face, blue-armoured, head-band covering a wound, with the host of
warriors, wild heads, grey and red head-cloths, white, black and brown
clothes, insignia on their clothes, bare legs, tall torch-staves, hand-bells,
noise. They creep up with outstretched staves and lights, attempt wearily
and angrily to restrain the on-storming adventurer, drag his horse down.
He moves forward. They break the circle around him, shouting with slow
crescendo.

WARRIORS
We were the wheel of flame around him,
We were the wheel of flame around you, stormer of sealed for-
tresses!
follow on hesitantly in a chain; he moves forward at the head with the
torch-bearer before him.

WARRIORS
Lead us, white-face!

While they are trying to drag his horse down, maidens with their leader
descend the ramp right leading from the castle wall.

WOMAN
red robes, flowing yellow hair, large
loud
When I breathe the blonde disc of the sun flickers.
My eye gathers up the rejoicing of men.
Their stammering desire creeps like a beast around me.

MAIDENS
break away from her, only now see the stranger

FIRST MAIDEN
inquisitively
Our Lady!
His breath hangs on her.

FIRST WARRIOR
thereupon to the others
Our master comes like the new day rising in the East.

SECOND MAIDEN
naively
When will she be embraced with bliss!

WOMAN
looks at the man fixedly
Who is the stranger who beheld me!

FIRST MAIDEN
points him out, screams
Banished boy-child of the mother of sorrows
Fled with serpent-encircled head.
Do you know him again?

SECOND MAIDEN
smiling
Bottomless depth wavers.
Shall she drive out the dear guest?

THE MAN
amazed, his column stops
What spake the shade?
raising his face to the woman
Did I discern you, did you stare at me?

WOMAN
fearing and longing

Who is the pale man?
Keep him back!
screaming shrilly runs back
You let him in, who senses our undefence?
The fortress gate gapes wide!
FIRST WARRIOR
Whatsoever parts air and water,
Bears skin or feather or scale,
Hairy and naked ghost,
Him they all must serve.
SECOND MAIDEN
Together tears and laughter crease her golden brow
Come, huntsman, catch us . . .
laughter
FIRST WARRIOR
to the Man
Embrace her!
The neighing drives the mare mad.
Put the thighs to the beast!
FIRST MAIDEN
slily
Our Lady is lost in the web of her thoughts,
Has not yet reached full shape.
SECOND MAIDEN
boasting
Our Lady rises and falls,
but never is brought low.
THIRD MAIDEN
Our Lady is naked and smooth,
but ever of open eye.
THIRD WARRIOR
scornfully to third maiden
Little fish gets caught on hook.
Fisherman hooks himself she-fish!
SECOND WARRIOR
to second maiden; he has understood
Hair tossed back! Her face freed . . .
The spider has climbed out of the web.

27

THE MAN
has lifted the woman's veil; angrily
Who is she?
FIRST WARRIOR
inciting
She seems to fear you, catch her!
Only fear enfeebles.
You must frighten what you capture!
FIRST MAIDEN
fearfully
Lady, let us flee.
Put out the lights of the leader!
SECOND MAIDEN
headstrong
Mistress, here let me await the day . . .
Bid me not go to bed
With longing in my limbs!
THIRD MAIDEN
pleading
He must not be our guest, breathe our air!
Let him not rest here this night
lest he affright our sleep.
FIRST MAIDEN
He brings no luck!
FIRST WARRIOR
She shows no shame!
WOMAN
Why do you bind me, Man, with your gaze?
Devouring light, you confuse my flame!
Consuming life floods over me.
Oh, take away the terrible hope—
THE MAN
starts up in wild rage
You men! Take hot iron and burn my brand into her red flesh!
Warriors carry out the order. First the band with the torches struggle with her, then the old man with the iron, tears open her dress and brands her.
WOMAN
screaming in terrible pain
Beat it back, the evil plague.

She leaps at the man with a knife and wounds him in the side. The man falls.

WARRIORS

Flee him possessed, strike dead the devil!

Woe on us guiltless, quickly bury the conqueror.

THE MAN

in agony from wound, singing with bleeding gash visible

Senseless lust from horror to horror,

Quenchless gyration in the void.

Gestation without genesis, sun's collapse, reeling space.

End of those who brought me praise.

Oh, your pitiless word.

WARRIOR

to the man

We know him not.

Spare us!

Come, you Grecian maidens, let us celebrate our wedding feast by his bier.

ALL MAIDENS

He terrifies us,

You we loved when you came.

The maidens lie down beside the warriors caressingly on the floor right. Three warriors make a bier from ropes and branches and put it into the tower with the man on it weakly moving. Women fling shut the grilled gate and go back to the men.

THE OLD MAN

gets up and locks it. All dark, little light in the cage.

WOMAN

alone, lamenting, defiant

He can not live, not die,

He is ghost-pale.

She creeps in a circle round the cage. Grabs compulsively for the grille. Threatens with her fist.

WOMAN

defiant

Open the gate, I must to him!

rattles in desperation.

WARRIORS AND WOMEN

disporting themselves, in the shadow, confused.

We have lost the key—we'll find it—Do you have it?—Did you see it?—it's not our fault. We know you not—What know we of ye! The conflict is incomprehensible and lasts an eternity.

Go back again. Cock-crow; it grows lighter in the background.

WOMAN

reaches with her arm through the gate, panting wickedly

White face! Do you start, know fear?

Do you but sleep? or wake? Do you hear me?

THE MAN

inside, breathing heavily, laboriously raises his head, later moves a hand, then both hands, raising himself slowly, singing, withdrawing into a trance.

Wind that sighs, time on time,

Solitude, peace and hunger confuse me.

Worlds swing by, no air, evening long draws on.

WOMAN

with beginning of fear

So much life pours from the split,

So much force out the gate,

Pale as a corpse is he.

creeps up the ramp again, her body quivering, again laughing loud.

THE MAN

has stood up slowly, leans on the grille.

WOMAN

becoming weaker, fiercely

Here in this cage I tame a wild beast,

Does your song from hunger howl?

THE MAN

opens his mouth to speak

. . . . . .

Cock-crow.

WOMAN

shivering

You, you're not dying?

THE MAN

powerfully

Stars and moon! Woman!

A singing being, bright shining

In dream or waking state I saw.

My breathing unravels dark things.

Mother . . . You lost me here.

WOMAN

lying on him completely; separated by the grille, she slowly opens the gate.

WOMAN

softly

Forget me not . . .

THE MAN

rubs over his eyes

Cankerous thought corrodes the brow . . .

WOMAN

tenderly

It is your wife!

THE MAN

gently

A sliver of shy light!—

WOMAN

pleading

Man!! Sleep for me . . .

THE MAN

louder

Peace, peace, delusion, leave me . . .

WOMAN

opens her mouth to speak

. . . .

THE MAN

lonely

I am afraid—

WOMAN

more and more violently, screaming out

I don't want to let you live. You!
You weaken me—
I kill you—you bind me!
I captured you—and you hold me!
Let go of me—you clasp me—as with iron
Chains—throttled—away—help!
I lost the key which held you fast.
lets go the gate, collapses on the ramp.

THE MAN

stands erect, tears open the gate, and with fingers of his outstretched hand touches the woman now stiffly rearing up in violent spasm; she is quite white. She feels her end, tenses her limbs, looses them in a slowly descending scream. The woman collapses and as she falls, seizes the torch from the old man, who is getting up. It goes out shrouding everything in a shower of sparks.

THE MAN

stands on the topmost step, warriors and maidens who try to flee from him rush screaming into his path.

WARRIORS AND MAIDENS

The Devil!

Bind him, save yourselves,

Each man for himself—lost!

THE MAN

goes directly towards them. He kills them like flies. The flame jumps over to the tower and rips it open from top to bottom. Through the path between the flames the man fast departs. Far, far away, cock crows.

AWAKENING

by August Stramm

1915

Translated by J. M. Ritchie

HE
SHE
IT (Girl)
HOTEL MANAGER
PORTER
MOB

Room in a hotel

Single beds side by side; on the opposite wall double doors; on the back wall between high windows a mirror. Valises and clothing scattered over chairs and bed-side tables.

SHE *in the front bed, sits up and stares into the dark.*

HE: *after some time*] Why are you awake?

SHE *switches on the light on the bed-side table.*

HE: *takes hold of her arm, tenderly, concerned*] Why are you awake?

SHE *rubs the sleep from face and hair, turns back the covers and pushes her feet into slippers on the floor.*

HE, *half sitting up, gazes intently at the back of her neck.*

SHE *presses her knees together and places her hands on them, peering round the room.*

HE: *sits up with a jerk, harshly*] What are you staring at?

SHE *mumbles unintelligibly, gestures round the room with her left hand, flings herself down again, and hides her face in her hands.*

HE: *stares around the room, looks at her, leans over to her, gently*] dreams . . . [*his hand caresses her neck*].

SHE *gives a convulsive start; her hands drop to the bed.*

HE: *reproachfully*] Child!

SHE: *breathes*] Don't touch me!

HE: *reassured*] Darling!

SHE: *horrified*] Don't touch me!

  HE *takes away his hand.*

  SHE *shudders.*

HE: *gently*] What's wrong?

SHE: *cowers away, arms crossed and hands on shoulders, drily, tonelessly*] I don't know.

HE: *in pyjamas, climbs into slippers, crosses to the door shaking his head and switches the overhead light on*] There you are! [*rushes about the room swinging his arms*] look! just take a look!

  SHE *lifts her head and peers around the room.*

HE: *stops centre between door and window and smiles at her with playful superiority*] See anything?

SHE: *motionless*] Yes . . . right there . . .!

HE: There's where *I* am!

SHE: *shudders*] Yes [*checks carefully and nods*] yes!

HE: *goes up to her tenderly*] You see.

SHE: *leaps up, wards him off, screams*] Stop! Stop! Stop there!

HE: *taken aback, returns to the spot reluctantly*] God!

  SHE *scrutinizes him silently.*

HE: *irritated*] It's stifling here! Let's be reasonable! [*goes to the window*].

  SHE *goes to stop him, loses interest and wilts, moves forward to the foot of the bed and bends over to look at the spot where he was standing.*

HE: *pulls the curtain and looks back*] Well? Something there?

  SHE *raises her eyes to gaze out the window and gathers her nightdress tighter round her body, shuddering.*

HE: *hand on the window-latch*] Feeling cold?

SHE: The night is wet.

HE: *stares at her disconcerted*] We are safe here! [*goes over to her and steers her towards the bed*].

SHE: *pushes him away*] No! No!

HE: You've had a bad dream.

SHE: *resists weakly*] I've been asleep.

HE: *sets her down on the bed*] Then let's go back to sleep.

SHE: *looks around the room, asserting with interest, not fear*] And there *is* something there!

HE: *impatiently*] What? What can be?

  SHE *gets up and looks curiously at the spot, gives a nod of confirmation.*

HE: *goes back and scrapes with his foot, roughly*] Where can there be anything?

SHE: *controlled*] Yes . . . exactly . . . where can there. . .? [*she glances in the mirror and puts her hair into place; stops short in horror*] And what do I look like? I look like! Oh!

HE: *crossly*] Leave the mirror alone!

SHE: *presses the palms of her hands against her temples*] That's not me.

HE: *steps in front of her and blocks out the mirror*] Who else?

SHE: *repeats after him*] Yes . . . who . . .?

HE: *explodes*] God Almighty! [*controls himself and stamps his foot*] Nothing!!

SHE: *stares at him horrified*] Nothing! Nothing!

HE: *controlled*] You're driving me mad too! Your illusion . . .

SHE: *with feeble resistance*] Illusion . . . illusion . . .

HE: *seizes her arm roughly and shakes her*] Be reasonable now.

SHE *screams and retreats from him in horror.*

HE: *lets her go and looks about him in helpless terror*] What? What?

SHE: *exhausted*] You are strangling me.

HE: *overstrained, weeps*] But I . . . I . . . absolutely not a thing . . . I . . . [*pleading before her with hands clenched fiercely*].

SHE: *stirs after some time, rubs her wrist, shivers feebly*] Yes! It is stifling here! Open the window!

HE: *beside himself flings round the room in a rage*] No! No! No! [*stops in the middle of the room*].

SHE: *with feeble firmness*] Open the window.

HE: *by the window, flings his fists apart as if bursting shackles*] Alright, damn you! [*fuming with rage, tears the window latch down with both hands*] Alright!!! [*the window collapses about him, the wall between the windows cracks wide open, the mirror shatters into the room*].

HE *rigid amid the collapse.*

SHE *horrified.*

HE: *turns the window latch over in his hand looking at it awe-struck*] Rotten!

SHE *whimpers.*

HE: *looks across to her hesitantly*] I didn't mean to do that! Oh!

SHE: *whimpers*] The mirror.

HE *starts, flings the lever into the debris and rears into wild laughter.*

SHE: *trembling in horror*] Oh! Oh! You! You! You're terrible!

Terrible! You!

Voices, shouts, people running about outside the house. Noises inside. The dust has dispersed through the great gap in the wall.

A star flares in the inky night.

HE *laughs more calmly and reflectively; the laugh ripples away into silence; then stands quite still and looks up at the star.*

SHE: *cowers horrified on the bed shaking hands clutching the bed-head and listening to approaching sounds at the door, babbles*] C . . c . . coming.

HE: *calm, dreamily*] See the star.

SHE *babbles unintelligibly.*

HE: Look though! The star!

SHE: *completely dissolved in horror*] Kn . . kn . . knocking.

Violent knocking at the door, shouting, door handle is rattled fiercely.

HE *steps unconcerned farther into the gap in the wall and gazes up at the star.*

SHE: *gives a start, hurriedly scrambles over to him, holds him back and babbles*] You . . . you'll fall! You'll fall!

Heavy banging, rattling at the door; shouts: Hey! Hey there!

SHE: *pulls at him, crawling backwards*] Listen! Listen will you!

HE *never takes eyes off the star.*

SHE: *leaps up and shakes him wildly*] For heaven's sake be . . .

Blows from heavy bar are heard against the door.

HE *comes to himself, turns to the door and puts his arm round her protectively.*

Running and shouting outside in the street.

The door begins to give under the weight of curses and blows.

SHE *clings to his breast unconscious.*

HE: *carries her across the rubble, looks up at the star, says regretfully*] Lost in the clouds!

The night turns black.

The door bursts open.

The HOTEL MANAGER *and the* PORTER *force their way in with crowbars, breathing heavily.*

HE *calmly lays her on the bed and tucks her in.*

MANAGER: *wildly threatening*] You!

PORTER *with upraised crowbar stares dully at the heap of rubble.*

HE *looks up calmly.*

MANAGER: *in front of the pile of rubble, beside himself with rage*] You're pulling my house down!

HE: *calmly*] I.

MANAGER: *beyond himself*] You you you! Lie! Lie! Lie!

PORTER: *threatens clumsily*] Fur chrissake!

HE: *calmly*] The wall has collapsed.

MANAGER: *beyond himself, repeating the words*] The wall! The wall!
The wall! [*screams wilder and wilder*] Godal! Godal! Godalmighty!
Police! Police! Police! I'll have you arrested! I'll have . . .

PORTER: *joins in*] Pleece, pleece.

HE: *gives a start, hurriedly*] But what if I [*makes a sign*].

MANAGER: *stares at him*] You you you [*gets the meaning and immediately changes tune*] What?

HE: *calmly*] Let's discuss this quietly [*signs for quiet*] my wife . . .

MANAGER: *suddenly all sympathy, puts down the crowbar and rubs his
hands together*] Oh!

PORTER *tugs off his cap in confusion and retreats slowly fiddling with
the crowbar.*

MANAGER: We c'n fetch a doctor [*turns to the PORTER who claps on
his cap and does an about-turn raring to go*] 'Kay.

PORTER: *raring to go*] 'Kay.

HE: *hurriedly*] No, no no stop! Many thanks! She'll manage
alright . . .

Noise and din outside in the street.

Muffled thunder in the distance.

MANAGER: *embarrassed*] Sure! Sure! [*looks out*] Take a look at that
mob, willya! [*to porter*] Get on down! Lock the door! See that
scum don't get in!

PORTER: *shifts his cap*] 'Kay [*hurries off in relief*].

HE *pulls his cashbox out from under his pillow.*

MANAGER: *follows his movements, with fawning servility*] You can
have another room . . . sir . . . sir! [*peal of thunder*] That storm.

HE *opens the box which is bursting with gleaming gold coins.*

MANAGER *blinded, gurgles and gulps in confusion, holding out his
hands for it greedily.*

HE: *counts a number of gold coins into the manager's hand*] Is that
enough?

MANAGER: *hopping from one leg to the other, stammers in the excitement
of his greed*] Come on. Come on.

HE: *firmly*] That is enough!

MANAGER: *hesitantly*] Aw no!

37

HE: *closes the strong box*] Yes.

MANAGER *firmly*] Naw naw naw [*seizes the box*].

HE: You!!

MANAGER: You!!

HE *tries to tear the box free.*

MANAGER: *holds on*] Get out of my way!

HE: Impudent wretch.

MANAGER: *tugs scornfully*] Okay young fella, just be quiet will you? Quiet now? Keep your trap shut young fella [*tries with all his might to tear the box away*].

HE: Ha!

MANAGER: I know! I know what's what! [*meaningfully*] Your wife.

HE: *furious*] Swine!

MANAGER: *laughs fiercely*] Yeh yeh [*the box gets opened in the tussle; the gold coins roll out into the night*].

MANAGER: *aghast*] Oh! Oh! The money!
Rumble of thunder.

MANAGER: Ooh! Ooh! That lovely money! Money! [*raises his fist against him, who is holding the empty box in perplexity*] You! You! *Din, screaming and scuffling outside.*

MANAGER: *trembling in all his limbs*] What a pig! What a pig! What a . . . [*hustles to the door*] Money! All that money! [*loses coins, picks up, drops more*] Oooh! [*makes a frantic rush out into the mounting din outside*].

HE *shakes the box to make sure it's empty and shakes his head.*
Lightning and loud thunder-clap.

SHE: *roused*] What was that? What was that?

HE: *calmly mocking*] Thunder!

SHE: *stares around*] Where am I?

HE: *as before*] Here!

SHE: *whimpers and listens*] Roaring of the river.

HE: Roaring of the rabble.

SHE: *excited*] That's water! Water! The river! We've crossed the river! Oh! So black! So black in the evening sun.
Wild screams, laughter, din, howls of derision, rattle of hailstones outside.

SHE: *hides in the bed whimpering*] What's got into the people? What's got into the people?

HE: *calmly, contemptuous*] My money

SHE: *horrified*] Ooh! Put out the light!

HE: *goes calmly to the door and turns off the light*] Yes.

Lightning, thunder and hail.

The flickering reading lamp lights the bed corner; the rest of the room is in darkness.

SHE: *weeps*] Oh! If only we were we.

HE: *interrupts rudely*] What we?

Horrible scream, then sudden silence outside.

HE: *gives a start and peers out, steps back hurriedly*] We can't stay here [*slips into his trousers*].

Wild screams outside and lamentations: Murder! Murder!

HE: *frantic*] Look! Get dressed? Get dressed? We must get away! Get away!

SHE: *hurries out of bed*] Darling, darling [*trembling in every limb*] if they if they if they find us here, if they [*leans against the wall exhausted*].

HE: *snatches up her things and throws them to her in the corner*] Quick, quick! No time.

SHE: *no will left, picks up her clothes—weakly*] Darling, darling [*lets her head fall back weakly*].

HE: *urgently pulls on his jacket*] Please please.

SHE: Darling I'm pregnant! I feel it!

HE stares at her.

Banging and shouting on the landing.

HE hurries to the door to lock it.

People crowd in at the door screaming.

HE leaps back into the corner by the bed, which is naturally barricaded off by the heap of rubble and places himself beside her protectively.

SHE by the window, hands supported behind her, stares at the intruders full of horror.

Workers, Tradesmen and Youths in the doorway are taken aback and fall silent at the sight of the couple, then step in carefully one after the other peering around lewdly.

Lightning followed by thunder.

THE CROWD: *moves closer lewdly*] Wow! Wow! Ooah! Ooah! Oh! Oh! Oh! Take a look at that ! Her nightie! Ooah! Shameless hussy! In a nightie! Ooah! [*lecherous hands lust*].

Some try to climb over the heap of rubble.

HE *rips open the drawer in the bedside table and pulls out a pistol.*

39

CONFUSION: *starts back*] Will ye look at that! The dog! He's going to shoot! Pleece! Pleece! The dog! The dog! The dog! Put it down! [*Surge backwards and forwards, jeering*] You! You! We'll get you! Kill 'm! The woman! The woman! His woman! His woman!

PEDLAR: *sneaks about*] What do you know! Well, look at that! Well well! Take a look at that! Strike me dead! Strike me dead! Strike me dead! She's Lumpel's wife! Lumpel's wife! Lumpel the business-man, his wife! His wife! From Bunzel street!

CONFUSION: *shouts*] From Bunzel street! From Bunzel street! Lumpel! Lumpel! Bunzel! Bunzel street!

PEDLAR: *shouts above the din*] Yeh yeh yeh! She's Lumpel's wife alright! I'd know her anywhere! His wife!

SHOUTING AND SURGING FORWARD: *held in check by the revolver*] Bastard! Swine! Women! What a dog! Get Lumpel! Lumpel! Lumpel!

SOME: *hurry away*] We'll fetch him! We'll fetch him!

BURST OF LAUGHTER] Give him a nice surprise! Give him a nice surprise! Lumpel!

SHE *on the verge of collapse.*

HE *puts an arm round her, holding the pistol at the ready in the other hand.*

EXCITED SHOUTING: *does not dare come closer*] Will you put that thing down! He'll shoot! He'll kill! It will end in bloodshed! Your life's not safe! Up here! Up here! Pleece! Pleece!

MEN, WOMEN, CHILDREN, YOUTHS: *storm through the doorway amid great din and shouting*] They're bringing him! They're bringing him! They're coming with him! They got him! They have him! [*mingled with lewd shouts directed to her*] Oah! Oah! Oah! [*frightened retreat as the gun is caught sight of*] Oh! Oh! Put it down! Put it down!

TWO POLICEMEN *lead in the porter hand-cuffed, followed by folk and din.*

PORTER: *rushes violently at him*] That's him! That's him!

POLICEMEN: *stop him*] Silence! Stop!

CROWD: *screams*] Grab him! Grab him!

SERGEANT: *enters*] Silence! Silence here!

All fall silent.

PORTER: *in wild excitement tries to tear himself free and fling himself at him*] That's him! That's him!

SERGEANT: *seizes him roughly by the scruff of the neck and shakes him*]
Who is?

PORTER: *wildly*] Him him him him.

SERGEANT: *shakes him*] Dog! Dog! You've killed the manager
[*agitation in the crowd*].

PORTER: *rebels*] Dog dog dog! Money money money! He has the
money the money the money.

CROWD *surge forward in agreement.*

SERGEANT: *calmly to him*] Put down the gun.

HE *lowers the gun.*

PORTER: *howls violently shaken*] I'm an honest man! I've not hurt
a fly! Not a fly! Always have been! Not a fly! What did he
what did he chuck the money down for!

CROWD: *agrees*] If somebody treats money like that! Money! Your
own people kill for it! Kill!

SERGEANT *puts his hand roughly over the porter's mouth and looks
around threateningly.*

All fall silent.

SERGEANT: *pulls out his notebook, gruffly*] Who are you?

HE: *calmly, evading*] Yes.

SERGEANT: *roughly*] Who are you?

HE *does not answer.*

SERGEANT: *steps closer*] Put that away!

HE *pushes the gun behind him onto the window sill.*

SERGEANT: For the last time! I'm asking who you are?

HE: *calmly*] I travel.

CROWD *agitated and murmurs.*

SERGEANT: *flares up*] For chrissake! [*controls himself*] Alright! What
do you travel with? What in? What for?

HE *does not answer.*

CROWD *becomes increasingly unsettled.*

SERGEANT: *furious*] Will you answer me? Will you? Is that your
wife?

HE: *cold, incisive*] Yes.

Thunder and lightning outside.

CROWD: *in shrill revolt*] That's not true! That's not true! He's
lying! He's lying! That's not his wife! That's not his wife! Not
his wife! His wife! [*surges forward threateningly*].

SERGEANT *keeping them back with out-stretched arms.*
HE *picks up the gun again.*
Thunder and lightning.

PROFESSORS, CIVIL SERVANTS, BUSINESS-MEN, ARTISANS: *shout in wild confusion and press closer]* She's my wife! My wife! My wife! She's my wife! My wife! Devil! Devil! My wife! *[the raised pistol time and again pushes back the threatening fists].*

PEDLAR: *forces through arms flailing and roars above the noise]* Be quiet! Not mad! Not mad! Just listen! Listen! She's Lumpel's wife! Lumpel the businessman, his wife! From Bunzel street! I know for sure! Bunzel! Lumpel! Lumpel! Bunzel!

SERGEANT: You whore!

CROWD: *catches on]* Whore! Whore!

PEDLAR: *laughs jeeringly]* His business is women! He travels in women! Women!

CROWD: *catches on, violently]* He steals women! Our women! Our women!

BLACKSMITH: *leaps forward]* He seduced my daughter! He seduced my daughter!

HIS WIFE: *holds him back]* Joseph! Joseph!

BLACKSMITH: That's what he looked like! That's what he looked like! It was him.

HIS FRIEND: *pulls him away]* Rubbish!

HIS WIFE: *hanging on to his arm]* Joseph!

VARIOUS PEOPLE *pull and shove the smith back into the crowd.*

WHORE: *leaps forward, hands on hips, laughs coarsely]* He's my lover! He's my lover-boy! That's who! You! Baby! You!

SERGEANT: *thrusts her back brutally and roars above the tumult]* Silence! *Searing flash of lightning followed immediately by deafening peal of thunder.*
Deathly silence for a moment, then the women give a screech and cross themselves.

SINGLE VOICES: He's driving us all mad! Nobody knows what he is! He makes the storm! *[swelling]* Storm! Storm! His fault! All his! The murder! The murder!

PORTER: *catches on]* It was him! It was him! It was him! He did the murder! He caused it! I didn't mean to! I didn't mean to! I didn't mean to at all!

CONFUSION: He's the murderer! Murderer! Storm! Storm! Our

houses tumble. Our houses collapse! Up! Up! Inside with him!
Inside! Prison! Prison! Hard labour! Hang him! Hang him!
Arrest him! Arrest him!

The pistol swings in a circle and holds back the frenzy.

SERGEANT: *draws his sabre, foaming at the mouth with rage*] Put that
gun down. You're under arrest! You're under arrest! You're under
arrest! In the name of the law law law! Disturbing the peace, the
peace! Disturbing the peace of the whole city!

Howl of approval.

SHOUTS: *penetrate*] We were sitting in the local! Quietly! I've had
to leave my drink standing!

PORTER: *through it all*] I couldn't help myself! I couldn't help myself!
I didn't mean to!

ALL: *surge up to him and ebb back*] Murderer! Murderer! House
wrecker! Murderer!

SERGEANT: *flailing blindly with his sabre at the pistol*] Put it down!
Put it down!

PORTER *struggles free and escapes.*

THE POLICEMEN *laboriously after him, hampered by the throng.*

*A female voice gives a long-drawn shriek from the door and paralyses
the din.*

Glare of fire flickers through the gap in the wall.

WOMAN: Let me through! Let me through! Let me through!
Lumpel struck down. Old Lumpel! A stroke! A stroke! Struck
him down like a sack of potatoes! Dead! Old Lumpel is dead!
The minute we told him! Told him quite quietly! He's dead! [*goes
up to her in mad rage*]. Your husband's dead! Your husband's dead!
Your husband.

The glare of fire gets brighter, sparks fly.

SHE *has started up in horror at the woman's screaming, then smiles
puts her arm round his neck and hides her face in his chest.*

WOMAN: *beside herself, in furious indignation*] She's laughing! She's
laughing! She's laughing! She's laughing!

COMMOTION: Something burning! Something burning!

SHOUTS: *outside and at the door*] Fire! Fire! The lightning!

Alarm bells start to ring.

Klaxons and fire-engines outside.

CONFUSION: *shouts*] Fire! Fire! The city hall is burning! The market
is burning! The street is burning! Everything is burning! Burn!

Fire! Fire! [*flight and dispersal*].

SERGEANT: *hurries off*] Have the house surrounded! Have the house surrounded!

WOMAN: Just look! Just look! She doesn't move! Her husband is dead! She doesn't move! Her husband is dead! The devil has her in his clutches! The devil! [*points in sudden illumination at him*]. He is the devil!

MEN AND WOMEN: *cross themselves*] The devil! The devil!

WOMEN: *scream outside*] Our children! Our children! [*more women hurry off*].

SHE: *listens giving a sigh of relief, breathes*] Children!

HE: *holds her tighter*] My child.

CONFUSION: He's set fire to the city! The city! The devil! Devil!

WOMAN: Get the minister! The minister!

VARIOUS: Get him to smoke him out! Smoke him out! Minister! Minister!

INDIVIDUALS *hurry off and bump into the girl.*

GIRL *comes in, holding two children of five and six by the hand.*

GIRL: *looking intimidated, steps forward*] You, you your husband is dead! Your children.

CHILDREN *look around curiously, cling tight to the girl and cry.*

SHE *struggles free from him and stretches out her arms.*

HE: *holds her with all his might*] You are lost.

CHILDREN: *see their mother and stretch out their arms shrieking*] Mother! Mother!

SHE *held fast by him tries with outstretched arms to reach the children.*

HE: Stay stay! [*holds her straining every nerve*].

SHE *pushes him back with wild shriek and collapses clasping the feet of her children.*

HE *stands stupefied and tautly strained.*

GIRL *gapes at him horrified.*

MOB: *fall on her with a howl of fury*] There she is! Hooh! Hah! We've got her! Right! Now! Grab her! Hey! This way! [SHE *is pulled to her feet*] Out with her! Out!

WOMEN: *punch the unconscious woman in the face*] Filthy bitch! Filthy bitch!

MEN: *push the women back*] Get away! Get away! We'll have some fun! Some fun! Some fun!

WOMEN: She is a whore! [*shout into her face*] Whore! Whore!

MEN: She'll have to be broken in! Let's break her in! [*trail, drag and push her to the door*] The town whore! Going to be the town whore! Right away! [*kick her brutally*] Hoppla! Hoppla!

THE CHILDREN *hang on to her screaming.*

HE: *has been standing there intent on himself, now leaps with a shout of rage over the barricade of rubble flinging the pistol away, snatches up the centre cross of the window frame and smashes it down among them*] Let go! Let go! Dogs! Scoundrels!

THE CROWD: *scatters in wild terror*] The devil! The devil! The devil!

THE CHILDREN *let go their mother in horror and flee screaming.*

THE GIRL *presses herself hard against the wall beside the door and looks at him with enormous staring eyes.*

HE *storms after the crowd, comes back breathing heavily, throws the remains of the smashed window frame away contemptuously; as he looks around it all comes back to him and he bends down to her who is lying in a cringing heap on the floor in the middle of the room.*

HE: *places his hand on her hair, tenderly*] Darling.

HE *tries to raise her up.*

SHE: *leaps up, twisting and writhing to get away, the palms of her hands extended against him in utmost horror*] Oh you! Oh you! [*utters a long-drawn scream*] Ooooh!!! [*raging violently hissing*] You! You! The walls crumble! You!

THE GIRL *presses her fists to her mouth.*

HE: *steps over to her soothing*] Strong strong!

SHE: *retreats from him to the door and clings to the door-jamb shouting back*] You here! You! You here!

HE: *leaps after her and seizes her wrist*] We'll escape we'll escape! We'll get through! Through the turmoil!

SHE: *writhes under his grasp and struggles, beside herself*] Through! Through! Through! Escape! Escape! Escape! God! Devil! Heaven! Fire! People! You you you.

HE: *holds her*] Be quiet! Be quiet! Quick!

SHE: *in utmost horror*] Whore whore whore! Wife wife wife! I will! I will! Will I! Whore whore whore! Not your wife! Never your wife! Your wife! Not [*tears free and rushes away drawing out the word in a long scream*] your wiiiiiife!

HE *stands, his empty hands open wide to receive her and stares after her, then turns slowly, head hanging, crushed; clenches his fists in a sudden fit gnashes his teeth, stamps over to the heaps of rubble kicks the stones as if they were footballs, laughs with hollow scorn out into the night of flames, his whole body trembling with rage, howling hoarsely.*

A GREAT BELL *strikes, rattles, gives a shrill jarring sound and dies with an almighty crack.*

Din, screaming, lamenting, steadily spreading fierce rain of fire] The church! The church!

HE: *leaps into the gap, props his arms against the walls and roars out with the power of fury*] Let the river in! Let the river in! Let the river into the streets! Into the gutters! Into the alleys! Let the river in! Open the dam! Open the dam! The devil! The dam!

THE SHOUT: *hurries further and further away into the distance outside*] The dam! The dam! The dam!

HE: *roars*] To the right! To the right! That's it! The sluice gates! Yes! Yes! That way! Idiots! That way!

WOMEN and CHILDREN: *wail*] Our houses! Our houses!

HE: *roars*] We'll build them again! Build again! Build them again!

CONFUSED SHOUTS: *outside*] Build! Build! Rebuild! Rebuild!

HE: *steps back over the rubble and laughs wildly, arms folded, nods in that direction and murmurs*] Rebuild! Rebuild!

Almighty rushing outside, foaming and hissing.

THE GIRL *pressed hard against the wall stands absorbed in him.*

HE *looks up, groans, sighs and glances around helplessly; his glance takes fright at the* GIRL.

THE EYES *of both stare deep into each other.*

HE: You? You? Who are you? Who you?

THE GIRL: *stammers confused trembling*] I . . . I.

HE *takes a step towards* GIRL.

GIRL *nestles against the wall stretching upwards.*

HE: What do you want here?

GIRL *stands fast staring at him.*

HE: *in front of the* GIRL, *looks into her face, astonished*] Aren't you? Didn't you bring?

GIRL: *calmly, in an undertone*] I am the sister.

HE: Sister?

GIRL: Her sister.

HE: Oooooh!! [*considers* GIRL, *after a while*] What do you want here? What's the matter with you?

GIRL: *coldly, dispassionately*] I don't know.

HE: Aren't you afraid?

GIRL *does not answer and stares at him.*

HE: Aren't you afraid? [*calmly with gentle mockery*] Heaven fire people! I caused the crime!

GIRL: *calmly*] I identified you.

HE *snaps upright.*

GIRL: You sir . . . my friend . . . built the church.

HE *stares and nods, folds his arms tight.*

GIRL: The city hall.

HE: *advances one foot*] You know that?

GIRL: *warmer, livelier*] The school! The dam!

HE *nods and rocks his body.*

GIRL: *exhausted, breathes*] I identified! Identified you!

HE: *steps even nearer to her, gently, hesitantly*] You? You? Sister?

GIRL *trembles.*

HE: *hard up against the* GIRL, *whispers hotly*] Sister?

GIRL *trembles and clings with great effort to the wall.*

HE: *bends over, without touching, his hands clasped tight behind his back*] You're afraid?

SHE *lays back her head and looks up into his eyes, her whole body trembling.*

The fiery glow outside dies down, distant shouting.

THEIR EYES *locked in each other.*

HE: *giving a sigh of relief*] She was awakened! Your sister.

SHE *spreads her arms wide against the wall.*

HE: *gently, groping*] Yes suddenly awakened.

SMOKE *devours the flames, hissing, roaring.*

The shouting comes nearer.

HE: You! You wake up! You! Wake up you! Do you hear! If . . . you . . . awake.

SHE *raises her hand silencing him.*

VOICES OF WOMEN and CHILDREN: *outside*] The master builder it was! That was the master builder! [*rejoicing*] Our master builder master builder master builder.

MEN'S VOICES *mix in, questioning, enquiring.*

HE: *gently seeking bemoaning*] Others.

WOMEN, CHILDREN, MEN: *call on the landing*] Master builder. Our master builder! Our master builder!

SHE *gives a start and places herself between him and the door pro-*

47

tectively.

HE *steps between her and the door, smiling looking over his shoulder to the door.*

SHE: *clasps her hands together and whispers looking up to him]* Husband!

WOMEN and CHILDREN: *storm in through the door]* masterbuil ... *[the word dies away in fixed stare].*

A LITTLE BELL *rings for matins.*

THE WOMEN and CHILDREN *cower down hands clasped.*

MEN *staring in at the door over their heads, take their caps off and stand mute in silent reverence.*

HE: *strokes her hair and lets his hand rest on her head, gently happy]* Wife! *The last red glow is extinguished, it grows quite dark outside.*

ETHEREAL NIGHT MISTS *waft in through the gap in the wall and dim the room.*

THE STAR *flares up brilliantly.*

HE and SHE *turn round slowly and arm in arm look up to the star in close embrace.*

THE GUARDIAN OF THE TOMB

1916

by Franz Kafka

Translated by J. M. Ritchie

Those taking part:
THE PRINCE
GENTLEMAN OF THE BEDCHAMBER
GUARDIAN OF THE TOMB
COMPANION OF THE HOUSEHOLD
THE PRINCESS
SERVANTS

Small study, high window, a bare treetop outside it; PRINCE *at the desk, leaning back in his chair, looking out of the window;* GENTLEMAN OF THE BEDCHAMBER, *with large white beard, by the wall near the centre door. He is youthfully squeezed into a tight jacket.*

Pause.
PRINCE: *turning away from the window*] Well?
GENTLEMAN: I cannot recommend it, your Highness.
PRINCE: Why not?
GENTLEMAN: At the moment I cannot formulate my misgivings with any precision. Though it is far from being all I want to say, may I for the moment simply state that commonplace on human behaviour about letting the dead sleep in peace.
PRINCE: That is exactly my opinion too.
GENTLEMAN: Then I have failed to grasp it correctly.
PRINCE: It would appear so. [*Pause*]
The one thing which confuses you in this affair is merely the peculiarity of my procedure in not simply going ahead with the new arrangement but announcing it to you beforehand.

GENTLEMAN: I must admit this announcement places a greater responsibility upon me, of which I must strive to show myself worthy.

PRINCE: Don't talk about responsibility. [*Pause*].

Well, to go over it all again: up till now the vault in Frederick Park has been guarded by one guard, who lives in a little cottage at the entrance to the park. Anything wrong in all that?

GENTLEMAN: Certainly not. The vault is over 400 years old, and has been guarded in this way for just as long.

PRINCE: It could be an improper abuse. But it is not!

GENTLEMAN: It is a necessary arrangement.

PRINCE: Well then, a necessary arrangement. Now I've been long enough in this country palace to gain insight into details which up till now have been entrusted to strangers—they prove to be reasonably satisfactory—and I have discovered that the guard up there in the park is not sufficient, there should also be a guard on watch down in the vault itself. It will probably not be a very pleasant charge. But experience shows that for every post willing and suitable people can be found.

GENTLEMAN: Naturally, everything your Highness disposes will be carried out even if the necessity for the new order is not grasped.

PRINCE: *irascibly*] Necessity! Is the guard at the park gate necessary, then? Frederick Park is a part of the castle grounds and is completely surrounded by them, the palace grounds themselves are abundantly guarded by the army, no less. What's the point of the special guard at Frederick Park? Is it not a mere formality? A comfortable last resting place for the wretched old man who keeps the watch there?

GENTLEMAN: It is a formality, but a necessary demonstration of the respect for the noble dead.

PRINCE: And a guard in the vault itself?

GENTLEMAN: Would in my opinion imply that you were policing it, which would be real guarding of unreal things, things removed from the human sphere.

PRINCE: In my family this vault is the border-line between the human sphere and the other, and on this border-line I want to place a guard. As to the, as you express it, necessity for policing it, we can cross-examine the guard himself. I have had him sent for. [*Rings*].

GENTLEMAN: He is, if I may be permitted the comment, a confused old man, completely out of hand already.

PRINCE: If that is so, then it is only further proof of the necessity to reinforce the guard in the way I have indicated.

PRINCE: The Guardian of the Tomb!

The SERVANT *leads in the guard, supporting him by the arm, as he would collapse otherwise. Old, red ceremonial livery flapping loosely on him, polished silver buttons, various decorations. Cap in hand. Under the gaze of his superiors he trembles.*

PRINCE: Onto the divan. [*The* SERVANT *lays him on it and departs. Pause. Nothing but a soft rattle in the* GUARD'S *throat*].

PRINCE: *in the armchair again*] Can you hear?

GUARDIAN *struggles to answer, but cannot, is too exhausted; sinks back again.*

PRINCE: Try to get a grip of yourself. We'll wait.

GENTLEMAN: *bending down to the* PRINCE] What information could this man give, credible and significant information at that? He should be put to bed as quickly as possible.

GUARDIAN: Not to bed—am still strong—comparatively—still hold my own.

PRINCE: That's as it should be. You are only just sixty. But you do look very weak.

GUARDIAN: Will soon have completely recovered—completely recovered.

PRINCE: I was not reproaching you. I am just sorry that you are so poorly. Have you any complaints?

GUARDIAN: Heavy duty—heavy duty—not complaining—but very weakening—wrestling matches every night.

PRINCE: What are you saying?

GUARDIAN: Heavy duty.

PRINCE: You said something else.

GUARDIAN: Wrestling matches.

PRINCE: Wrestling matches? What kind of wrestling matches, may I ask?

GUARDIAN: With your dead ancestors.

PRINCE: I don't understand. Do you have bad dreams?

GUARDIAN: Not dreams—never sleep any night.

PRINCE: Then tell us about these—these wrestling matches.

GUARDIAN *silent.*

PRINCE: *to* GENTLEMAN] Why does he not speak?

GENTLEMAN: *hurries over to the watchman*] Any minute might see the end of him.

PRINCE *standing at the table.*

GUARDIAN: *when the* GENTLEMAN *touches him*] Away, away, away! [*fights with* GENTLEMAN'S *fingers, then flings himself down in tears*].

PRINCE: We are torturing him.

GENTLEMAN: How?

PRINCE: I don't know.

GENTLEMAN: Coming to the palace, the audience, the sight of Your Majesty, the questions—his mind is not strong enough to stand up to it all.

PRINCE: *never takes his eyes off the watchman*] That's not it. [*Goes over to the divan, bends down to the watchman, takes his little skull between his hands*] Mustn't cry. Why are you crying anyway? We mean well by you. I myself think your job is no easy one. I'm sure you have earned the gratitude of my house. So don't cry any more and tell your story.

GUARDIAN: How can I, when I am so afraid of that gentleman there—[*looking threateningly, not fearfully, at the* GENTLEMAN].

PRINCE: *to* GENTLEMAN] You must leave if he is to tell us his story.

GENTLEMAN: But look your Majesty, he is foaming at the mouth, he is seriously ill.

PRINCE: *absently*] Yes, yes, go, it won't take long. [GENTLEMAN *leaves*].

PRINCE: *sits down on the edge of the divan. Pause*]
Why were you afraid of him?

GUARDIAN: *remarkably self-possessed*] I was not afraid. Me afraid of a servant?

PRINCE: He is no servant. He is a count, independent and rich.

GUARDIAN: Yet only a servant, you are the master.

PRINCE: If you want to put it that way, but you yourself said you were afraid.

GUARDIAN: I'd have to say things in front of him, which are for your ears alone, my friend. Have I not said too much in front of him already?

PRINCE: So we are confidants, are we, and yet I saw you today for the first time.

GUARDIAN: Saw me for the first time, but you have always known, that I [*index finger raised*] hold the most important post at court. Why, you have even given it public recognition by awarding me the Medal of Scarlet. Here, [*raising the medal on his coat*].

PRINCE: No, that is a medal for twenty-five years service at court. My grandfather gave you it. But I too will see that you receive an honour.

GUARDIAN: Do what you please and whatever corresponds to the importance of my services. For thirty years I've been your Guardian of the Tomb.

PRINCE: Not mine. My reign is scarcely a year old yet.

GUARDIAN: *lost in thought*] Thirty years. [*Pause*]
  [*Half-finding his way back to the* PRINCE'S *remark*] Nights last years there.

PRINCE: No report has ever reached me from your Department. What are your duties like?

GUARDIAN: Same every night. Every night it would nearly make you burst a blood vessel.

PRINCE: Is it only night duty then? Night duty for an old man like you?

GUARDIAN: That's just the point, Your Highness. It's day duty. A cushy job. You sit in front of the house door in the sunshine with your mouth open. Sometimes the watchdog puts its front paws on your knee and lies down again. That's all the variety there is.

PRINCE: I see.

GUARDIAN: *nodding*] But it has been turned into night duty.

PRINCE: By whom then?

GUARDIAN: By the Lords of the Tomb.

PRINCE: You know them?

GUARDIAN: Yes.

PRINCE: They come to you?

GUARDIAN: Yes.

PRINCE: Last night too?

GUARDIAN: Too.

PRINCE: What was it like?

GUARDIAN: *sitting upright*] Like always.
  PRINCE *stands up.*

GUARDIAN: Like always. Peace till midnight. I lie—begging your pardon—in bed and smoke my pipe. In the next bed my young granddaughter. At midnight comes the first knock at the window.

I look at the clock. Always punctual. There are two more knocks, mingling with the strokes of the clock and just as loud. These are no human knuckles. But I know all that and don't move. Then someone clears his throat outside wondering why I don't open the window after all that knocking. His Princely Highness may well wonder. The Old Watchman is still there! [*shows his fist*].

PRINCE: Are you threatening me?

GUARDIAN: *does not understand at first*] Not you—him outside the window.

PRINCE: Who is he?

GUARDIAN: He soon shows himself. With a bang the window and shutters fly open. I scarcely have time to throw the blanket over my little granddaughter's face. Storm blows in, puts out the light in a trice. Duke Frederick! His face with its beard and hair completely fills my window. Fantastic the growth over the centuries! When he opens his mouth to speak, the wind blows his old beard between his teeth and he bites into it.

PRINCE: Wait, you say Duke Frederick. Which Frederick?

GUARDIAN: Duke Frederick, just Duke Frederick.

PRINCE: Is that what he calls himself?

GUARDIAN: No, he doesn't [*fearfully*].

PRINCE: And yet you know [*breaks off*]. Tell me more.

GUARDIAN: Shall I tell you more?

PRINCE: Naturally, this affects me very closely, there has been a mistake in the allocation of duties here. You've had too much to do.

GUARDIAN: *kneeling down*] Don't take my post away from me, Your Highness. If I have lived so long for you, let me die for you too! Don't have the grave I strive towards walled up before my eyes. I am glad to serve and am still capable of service. An audience like today's, a moment's respite with my Lord, gives me strength for ten years.

PRINCE: *putting him back on the divan*] Nobody is taking your job away from you. How could I manage without your experience there! But I shall engage a second Guard and you will be a Head Guardian.

GUARDIAN: Am I not enough! Have I ever let one of them through?

PRINCE: Into Frederick Park?

54

GUARDIAN: No, out of the park. Who wants to get in? Whenever there's one of them standing at the railings, I wave my hand from the window and he runs away. But out, out, they all want to get out. After midnight you can see all the grave-yard voices gathered round my house. I believe it is only because they pack together so closely that they don't all come in through my narrow window with all their trappings. If it gets too bad, I fetch my lantern from under the bed, wave it on high and they scatter laughing and wailing, these incomprehensible beings; then I can still hear them rustling in the farthest bush in the park. But they soon gather again.

PRINCE: And they state their request?

GUARDIAN: At first they give orders. Duke Frederick especially. No mortals are so confident. Every night for thirty years he has been expecting to find me softened up this time.

PRINCE: If he has been coming for thirty years, it cannot be Duke Frederick; he died only fifteen years ago. He is the only one of that name in the vault.

GUARDIAN: *too much in the grip of his tale*] That I don't know, Your Highness. I never went to school. I only know how he always begins 'Old Dog' he begins by the window 'the Lords knock and you stay in your bed of filth'. You see, they are always angry about beds. And now every night we say almost exactly the same thing. Opposite each other, him outside, me inside with my back against the door. I say 'I'm only on duty during the day'. My Lord turns and shout into the park: 'He is only on day shift'. Thereupon there is general laughter from the assembled nobility. Then the Duke turns to me again: 'But it *is* day'. I reply shortly: 'You're wrong'. The Duke: 'Day or night, open the gate'. I: 'That's against my official instructions'. And I point with my pipe to a sheet on the wall. The Duke: 'But you're our Watchman'. I: 'Your Watchman, but engaged by the ruling Prince'. He: 'Our Watchman, that is the main thing. So open up, right away'. I: 'No'. He: 'Fool, you'll lose your job. Duke Leo has sent us an invitation for today'.

PRINCE: *quickly*] I have?

GUARDIAN: You. [*Pause*]

When I hear your name I lose my firmness. That's why I have taken the precaution of leaning against the door from the start, which is now about the only thing holding me up. Outside they are all singing your name. 'Where is the invitation?' I ask weakly. 'Bed bug,' he screams. 'You doubt the word of a duke?' I say: 'I have no instructions, so I'm not opening, not opening, not opening.' 'He's not opening,' the Duke outside calls, 'well then, press forwards all, the whole dynasty, against the gate, we'll open ourselves.' And in a flash the space outside my window is empty. [*Pause*].

PRINCE: Is that all?

GUARDIAN: What do you mean? Now my job starts. Out of the door, round the house, and immediately I bang up against the duke and immediately we are swaying in combat. He is so big, I so little, he so broad, I so slim, I fight with his feet only, but sometimes he lifts me up and then I fight the upper part too. All his companions make a ring round us and ridicule me. One of them, for example, slits my trousers up the back and now they all play with my shirt tail, while I fight. Incomprehensible why they laugh, for so far I have always won.

PRINCE: But how can you possibly win? Have you weapons?

GUARDIAN: I only took along weapons in the first years. What use were they to me against him, they only hampered me. We fight with our bare fists only, or rather really only with our breath. And you are always in my thoughts. [*Pause*]

But I never doubt victory. Only sometimes I'm afraid that the Duke might lose me between his fingers and he won't know any more that he is fighting.

PRINCE: And when is victory yours?

GUARDIAN: When morning comes. Then he throws me down and spits at me, that is his confession of defeat. But I have to lie there another hour, before I can really get my breath back. [*Pause*].

PRINCE: *stands up*] But tell me, don't you know what they all really want?

GUARDIAN: Out of the park.

PRINCE: But why?

GUARDIAN: That I don't know.

PRINCE: Have you never asked them?

GUARDIAN: No.

PRINCE: Why?

GUARDIAN: I dread it. But if you want me to, I shall ask them today.

PRINCE: *startled, aloud*] Today!

GUARDIAN: *in a matter of fact tone*] Yes, today.

PRINCE: And you can't guess what they want?

GUARDIAN: *thoughtfully*] No. [*Pause*]

Maybe I ought to tell you this as well. Sometimes when I'm lying there out of breath, and too weak to open my eyes, a soft being, moist and hairy to the touch, comes to me, a straggler, Countess Isabella. She feels me in various places, put her hand in my beard, lets her whole body glide over my neck under my chin and always says: 'Me, me, leave the others in, but let me, oh, let me out.' I shake my head as hard as I can. 'To Prince Leo to shake his hand.' I don't stop shaking my head. 'But me, but me,' I hear for a little longer, then she is gone. And my young granddaughter comes with blankets, wraps me up and waits with me, until I am able to walk. An extraordinarily good girl.

PRINCE: Isabella, a name I don't know. [*Pause*]

To shake my hand. [*Places himself by the window, looks out*].

SERVANT *through door centre*.

SERVANT: Your Highness, the Princess would like to speak with you.

PRINCE: *looks at servant distractedly; absent-mindedly to the Watchman*] Wait here till I come back. [*Exit left*].

Immediately GENTLEMAN *through door centre; then through door right,* COMPANION OF THE HOUSEHOLD, *young man in officer's uniform.*

GUARDIAN *as if he were seeing ghosts crouches behind the divan, gesticulating wildly with his arms.*

COMPANION: The Prince is gone?

GENTLEMAN: The Princess followed your advice and had him called.

COMPANION: Good [*turns suddenly, bending down behind the divan*]. So you miserable ghost, you actually dare to come into the royal palace. Have you no fear of the mighty boot which will kick you out of the gate again?

GUARDIAN: I'm, I'm—

COMPANION: Quiet, for the time being just be quiet, quiet, quiet, quiet and squat in that corner. [*To* GENTLEMAN] I thank you for the notification of the most recent princely whim.

GENTLEMAN: You made me ask him.

COMPANION: All the same. And now a word in confidence. Intentionally before that thing there. You, Count, are flirting with the other side.

GENTLEMAN: Is that an accusation?

COMPANION: For the time being merely an apprehension.

GENTLEMAN: Then I can reply. I am not flirting with the other side for I can't make it out. I'm aware of the under-currents but I don't dive in. I still think in terms of the open diplomacy we had under Duke Frederick. In those days at Court the only policy was service to the Prince. As he was a bachelor this was made easier, but it should never be difficult.

COMPANION: Very reasonable. Only your own nose—however loyal it may be—does not always show you the right path, only reason shows that. And it must make decisions. Let us assume the Prince is going astray—does one serve him by accompanying him on the way down, or by chasing him—with all due devotion —back again? Without a doubt by chasing him back.

GENTLEMAN: You came with the princess from another court, have been here only six months and you are ready to deliver the decisive judgment as to good or bad in complicated court relationships!

COMPANION: Blink your eyes for a second and you see nothing but complications. Keep your eyes open and you see in the first hour the eternally obvious as clearly as if you'd been seeing it for a hundred years. In this case it is true, the sadly obvious, which however, is now, we hope, approaching a favourable decision.

GENTLEMAN: I cannot believe that the decision which you wish to bring about and of which I have heard only a preliminary announcement will be a good one. I fear you have not under-stood our prince, the court, or anything here.

COMPANION: Understood or misunderstood, the present state of affairs is unbearable.

GENTLEMAN: It may be unbearable, but it springs from the very nature of things here and we would bear it to the end.

COMPANION: But not the princess, not I, not those who are on our side.

GENTLEMAN: What is unbearable as you see it?

COMPANION: Well, in view of the coming decision I will speak openly. The prince has a dual personality. One occupies itself with government and vacillates irresolutely in the eyes of the people, neglecting its own rights. The other admittedly seeks very closely for consolidation of its foundation. Seeks it in the past, and there deeper and deeper. What a complete failure to grasp the true state of affairs. A failure which is not without greatness, but the greatness is less than the error. Can that possibly escape you?

GENTLEMAN: It's not the description, it's your interpretation of it, I object to.

COMPANION: To my interpretation! But in the hope of gaining your agreement I have judged more mildly than I really think. I still withhold my judgment in order to spare you. Just let me say this—in reality the prince has no need to consolidate his foundation. Let him but use all his present resources of power and he will find that they suffice to do everything the most extreme sense of responsibility to God and man can demand of him. But he shuns balance in life, he is on the way to becoming a tyrant.

GENTLEMAN: And what of the humility of his nature?

COMPANION: Humility of one of his personae, because he needs all his powers for the second which is scraping together the foundation, which must be sufficient say, for the Tower of Babel. This work must be stopped, that should be the only policy of those who are concerned about their own personal existence, the principality, the princess and even perhaps about the prince himself.

GENTLEMAN: Even perhaps—you are very candid. To tell you the truth, your candour makes me tremble at the proposed decision. And I regret, as of late I have regretted more and more, being true to the prince to the point of helplessness.

COMPANION: Everything is now clarified. You are not merely flirting with the other side, you are even extending a hand to it. Only one hand, that is praiseworthy from the old court official. Yet your only hope is that our great example will carry you along.

GENTLEMAN: What I can do to stop it, I shall do.

COMPANION: I'm not worried any more [*pointing to the watchman*]. And you, who can sit so nice and quiet, have you understood everything that has been discussed?

GENTLEMAN: The Guardian of the Tomb?

COMPANION: The Guardian of the Tomb. You probably have to come from abroad to recognize him. Isn't that so, my boy, you funny old coot. Have you seen him yet flying through the

forest in the evening, so fast not even a crack shot can hit him?
But by day he cringes if you as much as look at him.

GENTLEMAN: I don't understand.

GUARDIAN: *almost weeping*] You are picking a quarrel with me, Sir,
and I do not know why. Let me, please, go home. I am not
something evil. I am the Guardian of the Tomb.

GENTLEMAN: You mistrust him?

COMPANION: Mistrust? No, he is far too insignificant for that. But
I want to put my hand on him. You see—call it a whim or
superstition, I think that he is more than a mere tool of evil, he
is quite a self-respecting, self-employed worker of evil.

GENTLEMAN: He has served the court quietly for thirty years, probably without ever having been in the palace.

COMPANION: Oh, such moles build long tunnels, before they ever
come out. [*turning suddenly to the* Watchman] First, away with
him—[*to the* SERVANT] take him to Frederick Park, stay with him
and don't let him out again till further orders.

GUARDIAN: *terrified*] I am to wait for His Highness, the Prince.

COMPANION: A mistake—get out.

GENTLEMAN: He must be handled with care. He is a sick old man and
the prince seems somehow concerned about him.

GUARDIAN *makes a deep bow to the* GENTLEMAN.

COMPANION: What? [*to* SERVANT] Handle him with care. But just
get him out of here. Quick.

SERVANT *about to grab.*

GENTLEMAN: *steps between them*] No, a coach must be fetched.

COMPANION: This is the real court atmosphere. I find it rather
tasteless. All right, a coach. You will transport this valuable item
in a coach. But now get out of this room, both of you. [*to*
GENTLEMAN] Your behaviour tells me—

GUARDIAN *collapses on the way to the door with a little scream.*

COMPANION: *stamps in anger*] Is it impossible to get rid of him?
Well carry him in your arms, if you can't do it any other way.
Will you at last get it into your head what is wanted of you.

GENTLEMAN: The Prince!

SERVANT *opens the door left.*

COMPANION: Ah! [*looks at the watchman*] I should have known,
ghosts are not transportable.

PRINCE *with quick step, behind him the* PRINCESS, *dark young lady,*

60

gritting her teeth together, stays at the door.

PRINCE: What has happened?

COMPANION: The watchman became ill, I was about to have him taken away.

PRINCE: I should have been informed. Has the doctor been sent for?

GENTLEMAN: I shall do so [*hurries out centre, comes back immediately*].

PRINCE: *kneeling down beside the watchman*] Have a bed made ready for him, fetch a stretcher. Is the doctor coming yet? Why is he taking so long? His pulse is very weak. Can't detect his heart beat. His poor ribs! How wasted away he is. [*stands up suddenly, fetches a glass of water, looking round*] Everybody is so rigid. [*kneels down again immediately, moistens the watchman's face*] Now he is breathing better. It won't be so serious, a healthy breed, does not fail even in extreme distress. But the doctor, the doctor! [*while he looks to the door, the watchman raises his hand and strokes the prince's cheek once*].

PRINCESS *looks away, goes to the window.* SERVANT *with stretcher,* PRINCE *helps to put him on it.*

PRINCE: Pick him up gently, oh you with your clumsy paws! Raise the head a little. The stretcher slightly nearer. The cushion further under his back. The arm! The arm, you are bad, bad orderlies. Wonder if you'll ever be so tired as this man on the stretcher. So—and now slowest possible step. And above all steady. I'll stay behind you. [*in the doorway, to the PRINCESS*] There's the Guardian of the Tomb for you. [PRINCESS *nods*] I had thought to show you him in different circumstances. [*after one more step*] You don't want to come along?

PRINCESS: I am so tired.

PRINCE: As soon as I have had a word with the doctor I shall come across. As for you, gentlemen, I shall expect a full report, wait for me here.

COMPANION: *to the* PRINCESS] Does your Highness require my services?

PRINCESS: Always. I thank you for your watchfulness. Never let it fail, even if today it was in vain. Everything is at stake. You see more than I do. I am always in my rooms. But I know it is getting blacker and blacker, this time it is an autumn sad beyond all measure.

THE PROTAGONIST

by Georg Kaiser

1921

Translated by H. F. Garten

CHARACTERS

PROTAGONIST
SISTER
FIRST PLAYER
SECOND PLAYER
THIRD PLAYER
THE YOUNG GENTLEMAN
INNKEEPER
THE DUKE'S MAJORDOMO
SEVEN MUSICIANS

Scene: Shakespeare's England

A hall in a country inn: bare, shabby, grey with dust. Doors left and centre. Right, four windows with tattered curtains; above, a musicians' gallery; rickety flight of stairs—up to it—skirting the windows. From left, INNKEEPER, and PROTAGONIST—in travelling cloak.

INNKEEPER: You could use the hall.

PROTAGONIST: *quickly crossing to the windows*] What's out there? The curtains don't close tightly.

INNKEEPER: Do you want to put the stage at that side?

PROTAGONIST: *glances out*] Your kitchen garden. Good. I just will not have any uninvited gapers.

At the centre door.

Where does this door go?

INNKEEPER: An empty room.

PROTAGONIST: *opens the door*] It will do for changing. Good again.

Beside the INNKEEPER.

All very self contained. I'd like to have the hall for three or four days.

INNKEEPER: You mean you're only going to play three or four times?

PROTAGONIST: Not for any motley crew driven together by their stupid lust for entertainment. We shall only rehearse here. Do you know if the Duke is in residence at the castle? What mood is he in? Has there been a death in his family lately?

INNKEEPER: He's hunting and in high spirits—with the sound o horns over the heath from morning to night.

PROTAGONIST: Excellent. I'll announce our presence to him by letter. Give me paper and ink.

INNKEEPER: You must let me see your papers.

PROTAGONIST: *takes them from the pocket of his cloak and hands them to him. Going to the door.*
Sister? [*he beckons*].

INNKEEPER: *looking up surprised*] You've got a woman with you?

PROTAGONIST: My sister.

INNKEEPER: In a company of players?

PROTAGONIST: Read the special license.

INNKEEPER: Since when in England are women allowed to—

PROTAGONIST: Never and nowhere, thank God. It would mean the ruin of the art of acting and turn the theatre into a brothel. The church would find it a reason for depriving us of the last grain of respect our talent compels. And rightly so.
Curtly.
My sister is on the road because I am.
Calling.
Sister!

SISTER *comes from left.*

PROTAGONIST: I'm in luck: the Duke is bound to be receptive. And before an audience like him I can drive my passion for transformations through the whole gamut from emperor to assassin.

INNKEEPER: Here, take your papers back. Everything's in order.

PROTAGONIST: *calling*] John—Christopher—Henry! Bring the trunks and scenery!

INNKEEPER: You appreciate my distrust of players. Your costumes aren't worth a farthing—you must pay for the hall straight away.

PROTAGONIST: What's your price?

INNKEEPER: Four shillings a day.

PROTAGONIST: *gives him money*] For four days then—and a reasonable room for the lady. Have you got one? Out of the way and with a safe lock?

INNKEEPER: I shall manage something, I suppose.

PROTAGONIST: *sharply*] Right now. The lady is tired.

INNKEEPER: I can't afford to sleep by day.

PROTAGONIST: Prepare some paper and ink for me in the public room.

INNKEEPER exit.

Vermin!

SISTER: Pay no attention.

PROTAGONIST: I'm thinking of you!

From the left the THREE PLAYERS with trunks and bundles from which poles are protruding. PROTAGONIST pushes back the THIRD PLAYER'S cap and pulls his long fair hair down over his forehead.

Henry, my tender dove and passionate mistress—

Patting the SECOND PLAYER'S cheeks.

Christopher—my faded lass cheated time and again but still full of desire—

Slapping the FIRST OLD PLAYER on the back—

and you, my John, prince of pranks and belly laughs: set things up in the backroom so we can enter by that door when we rehearse in a quarter of an hour's time. Tip the trunks up and lay out all the costumes, bright and dark. I shall choose from among my ideas when I return!

The THREE PLAYERS exeunt centre.

When is that rogue of a host in his pigsty of a tavern going to show you—

SISTER: I'm not tired.

PROTAGONIST: *embracing her*] Your forbearance annihilates me. I fall on my knees before you like the murderer before his victim whose dying eye lights the flame of forgiveness.

SISTER: *holding him tightly*] I am not your victim. I sacrifice nothing.

PROTAGONIST: Tramping the country roads in autumn wind and rain—eating scraps in wretched taverns—tossing on a filthy mattress among vermin—thrown to the scum of humanity with players!

SISTER: You are my brother.

PROTAGONIST: Sister, I couldn't bear the madness of these transformations which, today make me conquer the world as king—tomorrow press a blade into my hand against that king. When I'm playing I'm at the mercy of my part like a blind man at the edge of an abyss. I could not find my way back to myself—if you didn't call me brother. The lie of my playing is shattered in the lightning flash of that word—and quaking earth is steady again beneath my feet!

SISTER: I know, brother.

PROTAGONIST: I wouldn't be the player I am if I shunned the lie and failed to give myself up to every disguise with a surge of joy. Why do I sweep the audience off its feet as no other player has done? Why does their blood run cold? Why do their faces pale—and I write on this chalk wall before me letter upon letter spelling terror? Because I am the one who is acting on them. I am the one who laughs and raves with every pore of my skin—with every line of my hand. I am he, and he I remain and at the end I would make my exit, unable to strip off the character I was up there on the stage—I would create confusion that would end in horror—if I did not at last look into your face, the mirror of truth!

SISTER: *turning her head away*] Don't talk about it any more.

PROTAGONIST: Before you I must heap apology on apology!

SISTER: *feebly*] There is no need.

PROTAGONIST: And now the fever seizes me again. The play about to begin will change me into someone else, someone who will take over my personality. I am possessed by my part—I am still shaking with fear at falling into this frenzy—and yet I spur myself to the leap—because I can return to you—you standing before me without falsehood!

SISTER: What are you playing tonight?

PROTAGONIST: I shall spend myself utterly before a great Lord. The character does not matter. What counts is complete transformation!—Sister, I shall need you today as never before! Lead me after the play with a candle between us—its light must show me your eyes on which no shadow of a lie has ever fallen—or madness will seize me!!

He kisses her fiercely.

INNKEEPER *appears at the door.*

INNKEEPER: *sarcastically*] If the lady—I mean your sister—

PROTAGONIST: The letter for the Duke! Have you got a messenger who will deliver it in a civil manner?

INNKEEPER: The manner depends on the tip.

PROTAGONIST: Show the lady her room.

SISTER: Don't worry about me.

PROTAGONIST *exit.*

INNKEEPER: If you please, madam—

SISTER: Show the way.

Both exeunt. The FIRST PLAYER *throws open the door centre.*

FIRST PLAYER: *on the threshold*] Scullion!!— —Waiter!!— —Landlord!!— —Pack of thieving rogues and scoundrels—your tongue can be burning in the purgatory of the palate and not a single priest of the food and drink bearing fraternity comes to take pity on its craving! Gang of cutthroats—Must I go in my underpants — —?!

He slams the door, exit.

From the left the SISTER *returns hastily: stepping at once into the shelter of the wall. The* YOUNG GENTLEMAN *follows her immediately; closes the door behind him.*

SISTER: *staring at him*] Did you follow us?

YOUNG GENTLEMAN: *very calmly*] I had to—when you went away leaving my days empty and meaningless.

SISTER: You must forget— —

YOUNG GENTLEMAN: It can't be forgotten. This proves the worth of our betrothal and promises it will endure.

SISTER: You mistake what was a game—

YOUNG GENTLEMAN: For the truth that is now unshakably rooted within me. [*He bends over her hand*].

SISTER: *deeply confused*] Have you only just arrived?

YOUNG GENTLEMAN: My horses were faster and caught you up.

SISTER: Do you mean to stay—?

YOUNG GENTLEMAN: Until our union is formally sealed.

SISTER *looks at him. He embraces and kisses her.*

From secrecy—

SISTER: *throwing her arms round him*] Three nights of secrecy—

YOUNG GENTLEMAN: To a lifetime of light without fear or concealment!

SISTER: *drawing back from him with evident terror*] Has my brother seen you?

YOUNG GENTLEMAN: No.

SISTER: Don't let him see you.

YOUNG GENTLEMAN: Why not? Since I came with this purpose?

SISTER: That means nothing to him. But that there has been something— —

YOUNG GENTLEMAN: What do you mean?

SISTER: Going on—and that I have kept it secret from him— —

YOUNG GENTLEMAN: You mean, what has been between us??

SISTER: Not what has been! But that I haven't told him about you—and me—

YOUNG GENTLEMAN: It couldn't be told!

SISTER: I lied!

YOUNG GENTLEMAN: Such love can only start with a lie.

SISTER: That's not the point. He'll hear only the lie—

YOUNG GENTLEMAN: He'll hear and understand—

SISTER: Only the lie!—The lie on my lips—the lie in my eyes—the lie covering me from head to foot!

YOUNG GENTLEMAN: Will that be such a blow to him?

SISTER: It will strike him to the heart!

YOUNG GENTLEMAN: Should I act as though I were seeing you today for the first time. . . .

SISTER: He'll see right through us!

YOUNG GENTLEMAN: I can't understand your fear—

SISTER: Don't think about it. We must choose a moment when he is not himself—in a light-hearted mood—exuberant after the play—for after every play he lives on in his part for hours!

YOUNG GENTLEMAN: What's he playing now?

SISTER: He is letting the Duke choose the play. Then they'll rehearse here. Keep away from the house—

YOUNG GENTLEMAN: I'll be in the market-place.

SISTER: I shall join you there.

Listening.

To the market-place!

The YOUNG GENTLEMAN *kisses her, exit.* INNKEEPER *appears at the door.*

INNKEEPER: As for the closet—

SISTER *exit quickly.* INNKEEPER *follows.*

PROTAGONIST: *from the left, clapping his hands*] Hey, boy!

FIRST PLAYER: *sticking his head out of the door centre*] Is that the cue for ale and suckling pig?

PROTAGONIST: Right, John. This godforsaken hole is redeemed by a passable breakfast. Pheasant from the ducal hunt and burgundy from the barrel—

FIRST PLAYER: *slamming the door*] Henry—my trousers!

From the left the INNKEEPER *with the Duke's* MAJORDOMO, *magnificently dressed.*

INNKEEPER: Here he is before you.

MAJORDOMO: *to the* PROTAGONIST] The Duke has graciously received your letter and sends me, his Majordomo, to convey to you his admiration for the kingdom's greatest actor.

He bows formally.

PROTAGONIST: I thank you. Are we welcome?

MAJORDOMO: The occasion could not be bettered.

PROTAGONIST: Is the Duke going to choose the play?

MAJORDOMO: Tonight His Grace desires no more than the lightest entertainment. They are in a merry hunting mood and you have a chance to give full rein to your wit.

PROTAGONIST: The only way to raise a jest to the level of art.

MAJORDOMO: With one reservation: you must refrain from speech, for His Grace's guests from Spain and Germany would not understand your language. You are to perform a mime. To make plain the meaning will not trouble your exquisite talent.

PROTAGONIST: It will lead to quicker understanding—

MAJORDOMO: —if music explains your dumb show. I have brought His Grace's musicians.

He beckons behind the wings. The SEVEN MUSICIANS *enter with their instruments—bow.*

They are masters in the art of improvisation. They will be at your disposal for the rehearsal as long as you wish. Will you be ready tonight?

PROTAGONIST: Convey my acceptance and respect to the Duke.

MAJORDOMO *bow and exit. From the door centre rushes* FIRST PLAYER *still struggling into his coat.*

FIRST PLAYER: Spread the meal on the barrel right away and stop the clocks—I'll have breakfast and dinner in one!

PROTAGONIST: *stops him*] You'll play on an empty belly!

FIRST PLAYER: So now you want to—

PROTAGONIST: —make fun of you. I'll kindle my wit with the thought of your hollow guts!

FIRST PLAYER: Go and find your hungry muse—

PROTAGONIST: *sharply*] John!

FIRST PLAYER *is silent.*

Go back stage, John: put up the street—with the bright side to the front!

FIRST PLAYER *exit centre. To the* MUSICIANS.

Sit up there so you can keep your eyes on me during the play. Read the plot from my features and match your accompaniment to it. Don't spare the sharps—the play will not be lacking in spice either!

The MUSICIANS *mount the gallery and start tuning their instruments. From the door centre the* THREE PLAYERS *with the bundle.*

I'll invent the farce while I slip into my costume.

Exit.

The PLAYERS *now set up the poles and unroll two backcloths, showing house walls in garish colours with openings for doors and windows, facing one another at an angle. Above the gap between the two cloths they stretch a string bearing a board on which is written, 'A Street'; under it they hang a lantern. Then they bring two chests which they place behind each wall.* PROTAGONIST *from the back room: his supple figure in a tight-fitting costume of vivid silk; feathered cap and guitar.*

PROTAGONIST: Henry—you'll appear as the most ravishing girl. Christopher—dogs shall bark at your stale virginity. You, John, will be shapeless in a cowl. Play these parts—and afterwards, pheasant and burgundy!

THREE PLAYERS *exeunt.* PROTAGONIST *crosses to left, closes the door firmly, then turns round quickly to the gallery.*

The flute—excellent! Which of you plays the flute?

A MUSICIAN *stands up.*

Hold this tone and fasten it on the monk whenever he appears. It'll say more with its warbling than a thousand spoken words!

To the right, in order to close the curtain tightly.

Leave out the cello. We won't have anything serious. The tragedy introduced by your instrument is wiped from the world, and the last tear turned to sweet wine. You be the spectator—the only one I allow at the rehearsal—so that you won't take my

70

reproof for lack of respect!

Moving the sets.

One thing more: no overture! I detest a bill of fare in advance of pleasures to come. Besides, it hinders the inspiration that must spring from the spur of the moment. String pieces you have rehearsed together as the situation inspires. Agree about what you have to do and don't interrupt too often. You have been highly recommended!

The SECOND PLAYER *enters. He is dressed as a caricature of an old maid; however, he moves with the natural gait of a man.*

Christopher—you scarecrow, I shall be joined to you in wedlock such that even a bishop would grasp the reason for my extramarital escapades. Take your seat behind the window and shower me with caresses which soon drive me out of the house!

SECOND PLAYER *behind the left set—then at the window.*

To cure your jealousy completely will be the object of the farce!

To the MUSICIANS.

Blow the trumpet till the listeners' ears ache with the shrill notes like my skin does with the smacking kisses!

The FIRST PLAYER—*a fat monk—enters.*

You stay behind in the lane. I shall call you forth to help me get rid of my prudish wife. As a seducer you cut a ravishing figure!

The FIRST PLAYER *goes back. To the* MUSICIANS.

Don't forget the flute for him!

The THIRD PLAYER—*as a fair young maiden—enters.*

You're living in the house opposite and we have a long-standing agreement through glances from window to window. After some obstacles which we overcome with the help of the monk, we are united.

The THIRD PLAYER *disappears behind the right set—then appears at the upper window. To the* MUSICIANS.

In the meantime fetch from your fiddles a music sweeter than honey!

FIRST PLAYER: *coming to the front*] What's the band for? Are we to sing?

PROTAGONIST: Did I forget to tell you the most important thing? Not a word must be spoken—but our gestures will make plain what cannot be said!

To the MUSICIANS.

Strike up!

He pushes the FIRST PLAYER *back into the lane and steps behind the left set.*

Music.

The Mime has the following plot: The wife left turns back and entices her husband with languishing gestures. The husband comes eventually and suffers her caresses reluctantly. Then he conveys to her that he must go out. The wife grows desperate but calms down in the end. The husband disappears and steps out of the door below, locking it. The wife hangs out of the window and implores him to stay. The husband points to the lane through which he must leave. The wife throws kisses after him. Husband exit. The wife, overcome with grief, lays her head down on the window sill. After a while the husband returns, steals under the window right and begins a serenade. The girl's attention is caught and she looks down bashfully. The wife left listens— looks up—sees her husband and starts raving. The girl sits rigid once more. The husband runs under the window left and tries to pacify the wife. The wife threatens terribly at the opposite window. The husband sits down sadly beside the door—listens—and leaps into the lane from which he pulls the monk. He makes violent gestures at him—points to his wife and hands him the key of the door. The monk finally enters chuckling. The wife turns round, changes her attitude and waits humbly. The monk appears at her side; after some pious advances he grows importunate. The wife still resists. The husband returns under the girl's window and throws his guitar up to her. The girl fastens the latchkey to the ribbon and lets it down. The husband unlocks the door, enters and appears beside the girl. Love-play intensifying fast. At the other side the monk and the wife similarly engaged. Eventually one group catches sight of the other. The wife pushes the monk away and threatens her husband. The husband replies, pointing to the monk. The wife starts beating the monk. The monk disappears, the wife follows him. The monk comes out of the door, the wife after him, and flees down the lane. The wife knocks at the door right. The husband and girl, embracing, lean out and jeer at the wife. The wife grows tame and implores the husband to come down. The husband points at the girl whom he will bring home with him. The wife agrees. Husband and girl disappear from the window and come out of the door. The husband kisses alternately wife and girl. The monk appears from the lane in order to claim his rights from the wife; he is beaten by both

72

wife and husband and put to flight. The husband sends wife and girl behind their respective windows. Then he runs from one house to the other bestowing caresses on both.

SISTER *from left, quickly approaching the stage.* PROTAGONIST *sees her, runs up to her and embraces her fiercely. The music plays a jubilant finale.*

FIRST PLAYER: *running to the front*] I've got my beating—you've got your kisses: has ever a breakfast been more honestly earned?

PROTAGONIST: Put the innkeeper in the barrel right up to his neck if he spills one drop on the floor—pinch the fat thighs of the wenches if they serve you a lean pheasant!

He throws his purse to the FIRST PLAYER.

The THREE PLAYERS *quickly exeunt into the back room.*

Sister—merriment spans the earth like a rainbow. Instead of drooping the weeping-willows shoot upwards to where the clouds are suffused with the roseate sun. Melancholy in your eyes? Leda cuts her way through a flood of tears.

SISTER: Is it a merry play?

PROTAGONIST: What play? I'm in love. A lover with every nerve of my body. Did the earth not fall in love with the moon? If it didn't, I am a failure. The protagonist no longer changes the world—let the musicians strike up the dread finale.

SISTER: I'm in love as you're in love!

PROTAGONIST: Splendid, sister! What's worth anything but love? A curse on Atlas if he carried any but lovers!

SISTER: Brother, I'm in love!

PROTAGONIST: Sister, you lie. Where's your lover? There's nothing between your arms. Where's a character to hold you in fond embrace? Your limbs are empty of love, your lips devoid of kisses. You sad figure without secret fire!

SISTER: I'm loved in return!

PROTAGONIST: A lie without the shadow of a proof. You quit the stage of merriment empty-handed. Where's your lover?

SISTER: Will you call him?

PROTAGONIST: I'll call anyone. I'll spur on any stable lad who desires you. Love blasphemes love and purifies love with love!

SISTER: Don't change your costume before I come back!

Exit.

The MUSICIANS *have left the gallery and approach the* PROTAGONIST.

PROTAGONIST: Clasp your instruments in your arms till tonight. You're in love with one another. I know. You haven't played your flute you've kissed it—it was your fiddle's wedding-night with you. Your trumpet cried out with desire almost beyond fulfilment. That's the right sort of music when the player is played by his instrument and his craft is transformed into music of the soul. I dismiss you from the casual love-adventure we just performed into the infinite madness of all love-struck wit!

The MUSICIANS *bow and are about to leave left. The* MAJORDOMO *enters and, beckoning to the* MUSICIANS *to stay, approaches the* PROTAGONIST.

Are you swinging to and fro like a pendulum on the thread of your impatience? You're late, we have finished. Moreover, you wouldn't have been admitted. So you haven't missed anything!

MAJORDOMO: *shaking his head*] I'm here again with a message from His Grace.

PROTAGONIST: *with exaggeration*] He's too gracious.

MAJORDOMO: The unforeseen arrival of a kinsman, the bishop, necessitates a change of programme. The bishop would take little pleasure in a spicy jest. It would also do little to commend you further. His Grace wishes you to present a serious play. Is there time to rehearse it?

PROTAGONIST: *stares at him. His features grow hard—his body stiffens.*

His Grace would regret a refusal. You would miss an opportunity which might be of service to you.

The FIRST PLAYER *enters from the door centre—about to go left.*

PROTAGONIST: *harshly to him*] Turn round the sets. The rehearsal was a mistake. It must end in horror!

To the MAJORDOMO.

The Duke and the bishop shall gaze into the rolling eyes of madness!

Exit quickly centre.

The FIRST PLAYER *now turns the sets round: two dark house walls.*

MAJORDOMO: *to the* MUSICIANS] Go to your places and again follow the new directions exactly. This unique player's acting and your illustrative accompaniment will produce an extraordinary event, of the kind His Grace justly expects of such an alliance.

The MUSICIANS *once more mount the gallery and tune up. The*

MAJORDOMO *watches for a moment the* FIRST PLAYER *who busies himself sighing—then exit left. The* PROTAGONIST—*comes from the centre—he has changed into black, with a dagger in his belt.*

PROTAGONIST: *to the* FIRST PLAYER] Dress up as the others tell you. I've already told them the plot.

FIRST PLAYER *exit.*

Stepping under the gallery] You haven't touched the cello, now you shall make amends for your idleness. Carry through your cantabile without a break—

Turning to the other MUSICIANS.

—and arrange the full music in such a way as to make it sound like a faithful repetition of your previous accompaniment—only transposed into tragedy. For as every jest can be taken in earnest, we are not going to act a new play but simply transform our comedy into tragedy. Arrange it among yourselves!

The MUSICIANS *bow. The* SECOND *and the* THIRD PLAYER—*dressed as women in black—enter the door centre and go at once to their places behind the windows. The* PROTAGONIST *claps his hands towards the* MUSICIANS *and steps behind the set, left.*

Music.

The Mime: The wife left glances longingly and cautiously into the street; suddenly she sits up rigid. At once the husband appears and covers her with caresses. The wife refuses wearily. He is desperate. The wife pretends to be sleepy. Eventually the husband leaves her and rushes from the house. He behaves as if crazed with grief. Then the wife sees the girl right—and after a final sorrowful gesture towards the wife left, who seems to have fallen asleep with her head on the window sill, he knocks at the door right. The girl looks from the window, nods, and lets down the key on a string. The husband opens—rushes in, appears above beside the girl whom he covers at once with kisses as though trying to save himself from himself. From the lane appears the FIRST PLAYER *as a wealthy, elderly roué. He steals under the window left, pulls the key from his pocket, unlocks the door and enters. Above he appears beside the wife, whose neck he kisses. The wife starts up and throws her arms round him passionately. Unrestrained caresses follow. The husband on the other side tears himself from his frenzy, notices the love-play of his wife with the gentleman. Disappointment, offence and anger rage in his face. The girl wants to draw him back again—he remains rigid. Then he pushes back the girl, disappears and*

steps out below. He slips close to the house wall up to the door left—unfastens his dagger—and tries to open the door; it is locked. He stands paralysed and listens to the kisses above. This rouses him once more: he rattles at the door violently, leaps back and threatens them from below. The couple above start, the husband points to the door—the two above are utterly confused. This confusion grows in such a way that the two players do not know how to continue the play. They lean out of the window and ask the PROTAGONIST *for instructions. The latter goes on acting in a frenzy: he threatens with the dagger, runs against the door. The player right has also got up and fails to understand. The music, too, grows confused—breaks off.*
SISTER *from left.*

PROTAGONIST: *rushing towards her*] Who is it?! Who intrudes?!

SISTER: *throwing herself at him*] Happiness is upon me! I have known love, brother. Days of love have flooded over me!

PROTAGONIST *is motionless—mute.*

Why don't you laugh? Why don't you call for the man I have hidden from you till now? It will surpass all your curiosity—how we've loved and love still without end!

PROTAGONIST: You and who—??

SISTER: *lets him go—still laughing.*] We've been secret lovers—and so wrapt in secrecy that not even you found out. That'll make you laugh at yourself now— —
She checks herself— — looks at her brother closely — — looks round — — understands.

PROTAGONIST: Who laughs — — if he has been tricked by a whore?!

SISTER: *with a scream*] Brother—I lied only once!!

PROTAGONIST: The first lie breeds swarms of filthy lies — — it must be crushed at birth!!
He thrusts the dagger into her throat.
SISTER *sinks to the floor—dies.*

FIRST PLAYER: *runs to the door left—shouts into the wings*] A surgeon!!
To the YOUNG GENTLEMAN *who appears on the threshold.*
Are you a surgeon?

YOUNG GENTLEMAN: *to the* PROTAGONIST] How could you so take leave of your senses!
Kneeling down beside the body.
The INNKEEPER *enters.*

INNKEEPER: Damned scum. Off to prison!

Exit.

The MUSICIANS *have descended silently from the gallery and try to slip past.*

PROTAGONIST: *stopping them*] Go—and tell your master to spare me from arrest until tonight: he would deprive me of my best part where there is no longer any distinction between real and feigned madness. The bishop and the Duke will relish the spectacle!

METHUSALEM

or

The Eternal Bourgeois

A satirical drama

by

Iwan Goll

with three figurines

by

Georg Grosz

Translated by J. M. Ritchie

PREFACE

Aristophanes, Plautus, Molière, had an easy time of it; they got their best effects by the simplest means in the world: beatings. We have lost this sort of naïveté. The clown in the circus and Charlie Chaplin in the cinema still hand out kicks and punches, etc., but these are the points where the audience laughs least. Lack of primitive naïveté? Or is our more refined ethos to blame? This is certainly the case: but is the plebs also so refined? Even in army barracks physical punishment is frowned upon: this was not the case in the times of Aristophanes and Molière. And besides, modern man is now-a-days much more liable to have a gun than a stick. But a gun-shot is not so funny as a simple beating.

So the modern satirist must look for new stimuli. These he has found in Surrealism and Alogic. Surrealism is the most forceful negation of realism. Surface reality is stripped away to reveal the Truth of Being. 'Masks': crude, grotesque, like the emotions they express. No more 'heroes', just people, no more characters, just naked instincts. Quite naked. To know an insect you must dissect it.

The dramatist is research-scientist, politician and legislator; as surrealist he reports on these things from a distant realm of truth. These things he learns by listening at the impenetrable walls of the world.

Alogic is to-day the most intellectual form of humour, and therefore the best weapon against the empty clichés which dominate all our lives. Almost invariably the average man opens his mouth only to set his tongue, not his brain, in motion. What is the point of talking so much and taking it all so seriously? Moreover the average man is so sensitive that he takes any highly flavoured word for an insult and will throw death into the scales to avenge it. Dramatic alogic must ridicule all our banalities of language, exposing the basic sophistry of mathematical logic and even dialects. At the same time alogic will serve to demonstrate the multi-hued spectrum of the human brain, which can think one thing and say another and leap with mercurial speed from one idea to another without the slightest ostensibly logical connection.

But to avoid being a moaner, a pacifist and Salvation Army type, the author must perform a few somersaults, that you all may become as little children once more. For what is he after: to present you with dolls, to teach you to play, and then to scatter the sawdust from the broken dolls to the four winds again.

Plot of the drama? Events are so powerful in themselves that they contain their own intrinsic drive. A man is run over: an experience hurled hard and irrevocable into the stream of life. Why is only the death of man called tragic? A conversation five sentences long with an unknown woman can well become far more tragic for you in eternity. Drama should be without beginning or end, like everything else here on earth. But sometime it has an end—why? No, life goes on, everyone knows that. The drama stops because you have tired, grown old in a single hour, and because truth, the most potent poison for the human heart, may only be swallowed in very small doses.

Berlin 1922

Figures

METHUSALEM
AMALIA, his wife
FELIX, his son
IDA, his daughter
THE STUDENT
AUNT EMMA
MR. and MRS. ENTERITIS
MR. and MRS. BELLÉ
MR. and MRS. KINGDUMBCOMBE
PORTRAIT OF GRANDMOTHER
THE JOKE BOX
THE COCOTTE, VERONICA
A MAID-SERVANT
CROWD
BEAR
MONKEY
STAG
DOG
CAT
CUCKOO
PARROT

I

Methusalem, the original bourgeois, is seated in a large plush arm-chair, smoking a fat cigar, buried under a pile of larger-than-life newspapers. He has the gout and his right leg is wrapped up in woollen bandages. His face is dark red, fat bald head, tiny eyes, clean-shaven. Across his belly stretches a solid copper watch-chain as thick as a small hawser, with a miniature safe as a charm on it. As tie-pin, a golden shoe the size of a pocket-watch: the trade-mark of his shoe factory.

Amalia Methusalem, the essence of bourgeois house-wifery, wearing a rich dress with a long train, all silk and fine lace, much diamond and pearl jewellery round her neck and on her hands; fat, bulging breasts; and over it all a filthy kitchen apron.

METHUSALEM: *asleep, awakes with a start*] Nothing new. The world's getting so old.

AMALIA: Life is hard.

METHUSALEM: It's much of a muchness.

AMALIA: No juicy little murder in the paper?

METHUSALEM: Seven-and-six.

AMALIA: Spaghetti?

METHUSALEM: No, vegetable oil.

AMALIA: If only you could get celluloid umbrellas.

METHUSALEM: Is it goulash tonight?

AMALIA: Miserable spring: the carrots are so dear!

METHUSALEM: What's the time?

AMALIA: Quarter to.

METHUSALEM: You've always got to lie. Wicked woman, it's half past!

AMALIA: There's no parsley left in nature.

METHUSALEM: Is the new maid a blonde?

AMALIA: That would suit you fine, you brute. A pound a month she's asking.

METHUSALEM: *yawns*] To be or not to be.

AMALIA: Don't talk rubbish.

METHUSALEM: *with paper, turning over the pages*] A robbery with manslaughter!

AMALIA: Where? Read it out! Quick!

METHUSALEM: She was lying stark naked at the door.

AMALIA: The cheek of it.

METHUSALEM: Half an udder cut off.

AMALIA: All for love: oh, love!

METHUSALEM: *sings the song*] . . . is a heavenly POW-ER!

AMALIA: Nobody would ever think of murdering me for love . . . Can you understand that?

METHUSALEM: When's that goulash coming? [*turning pages*] They're going to tax drinking water!

AMALIA: We'll all die of thirst! Go bankrupt! Anybody else died?

METHUSALEM: Pee-wee from the Post Office.

AMALIA: What? What a dirty trick, to die at this time of year!

METHUSALEM: Fire Brigade Band's playing at the funeral. He always was an art lover!

AMALIA: It's too soon for winter hats. What ever shall I wear to the funeral! Fancy going and dying just like that—just tactless.

METHUSALEM: Time for my dose of salts. [*piano can be heard from the next room*].

AMALIA: *listening*] A genius, our Ida.

METHUSALEM: So she should be at a pound a lesson.

AMALIA: She'll marry a rich man.

METHUSALEM: So she should do, with parents like she's got. Ooh, my leg!

AMALIA: If she could only bake a cake!

METHUSALEM: And our Felix! Hi, hi! My son Felix. The pride of all the shoe-factories in Germany. The backbone of the Box-Calf Trust. Deserves a medal. Have you seen his new pinstripe trousers? Simply colossal!

AMALIA: *runs out*] The goulash, the goulash has caught!

METHUSALEM *falls asleep and snores. He dreams. On the window screen we see his dreams passing quickly in review.*

1st *Dream. Methusalem in a busy street. He is following a lady. Following his eyes, the film shows, first, her feet, in elegant shoes, then her legs, then her veiled face. She smiles. He takes her by the arm. They both enter a restaurant. While he is ordering the meal and the waiter serves it, the woman's face changes: Anna the cook is sitting opposite Methusalem. He pays no attention and speaks on importantly. Every minute the woman at Methusalem's table changes: a prostitute, then the wife of a business friend, his typist, his own wife twenty years younger, another prostitute, his daughter Ida, a chambermaid from the Hotel Excelsior—Methusalem talks earnestly to them all. They embody his experiences. A text-bubble appears in the film fluttering from his mouth:*

> 'Oh, my darling, no matter who,
> Be to me faithful, be to me true,
> Always wear a Methusalem shoe.'

2nd *Dream. A theatre. Poster: '"Hamlet"—To-day'. Methusalem goes in. The grave-digger scene is being enacted. Methusalem advances to the stage, climbs up and strikes the skull from Hamlet's hand. Text-bubble from his mouth:*

> 'Stop this blah, blah, stop this talk
> The dead can fly
> But Man must walk.'

Gives him a sparklingly polished lady's shoe. 'Why don't you make a

monologue about my goods? I'll give you 15 per cent off the store price.'
*3rd Dream. Methusalem as General. Parade. Only the symmetrical
marching boots of the soldiers are to be seen. Then he appears at the
head of the column and makes his announcement.* 'The whole army has
corns. We shall introduce the Methusalem shoe with the Toreador
Trade Mark. Methusalem's "National" Shoe Polish will give glitter
to the nation. Our future rests on rubber soles. Hurrah! Hurrah!
Hurrah!'

End of Film

METHUSALEM *wakes from his dream, bathed in sweat, snorts, groans,
wriggles about restlessly. Suddenly an idea occurs to him. He goes to the*
JOKE BOX, *which is the size of a normal chocolate machine, but it is in
the form of a man in tails, white tie, top hat, etc.* METHUSALEM *winds
him up painfully, inserts a coin between his lips, whereupon the robot
moves with little steps and arm movements and tells jokes in a
mechanical voice.*

JOKE BOX: Good answerrr! Moses Levy meets Mikosch in the street
  and says: 'How are you, Your Highness? What's new?' Mikosch
  answers: 'An ass and a Jew are being burned in Jerusalem to-day.'
  Moses Levy says: 'Lucky for us that we're neither of us there,
  sir.' Next joke! Called conscientiousss Janosch.

METHUSALEM: Ha, ha, ha! Well said, Moses! That's a real joke!

JOKE BOX: Janosch wanted to go hunting and he commissioned his
  butler to wake him at four. The butler wakes him up at three
  o'clock. Question? 'Why are you waking me up already?'
  Answer: 'Just wanted to tell you, sirrr, you can sleep a little
  longer yet!'

METHUSALEM: Ha, ha, ha! Oh, No! He's a genius, that Moses Levy!
  The machine runs down and stops in a grotesque position. METHUSALEM
  has meanwhile fallen asleep again. Darkness.

II

The Revolution of the Beasts

*The same scenery, but sulphurous yellow lighting. Methusalem is asleep,
buried under newspapers. The artificial or stuffed animals in the room*

begin to come to life and move. The dog at Methusalem's feet. The bearskin rug which lay in front of the table. The parrot in his cage. The cuckoo from the cuckoo-clock. The stuffed monkey. The cat at the window. The stag's head over the door. They all step out of their unnatural positions and move about the stage freely.

PARROT: Brotha, brotha, are you tha'?

CUCKOO: You're driving me cuckoo with your brotherhood.

A German Nationalist Bird sings 'Es braust ein Ruf wie Donnerhall'.

PARROT: Liberté. Egalité. Fra . . . fra . . . fra

CUCKOO: Phrases. Stupid, empty phrases! Must be a Jew with a beak like that!

PARROT: Excuse me, I am a Theosophist, Monist and Freudian. What are you?

CUCKOO: I am related to the Imperial Eagle.

DOG: Man is the crown of creation!

STAG: A turd in the hand is worth two in the bush.

BEAR: Si-lence!

Who dares defend mankind there?

Eat him up, eat him up quick!

Down with the enemy, down with man.

Forwards, back! Forwards, back!

Peace in our time.

Passengers are requested not to project . . .

Raise your legs gentlemen:

Skaal!

MONKEY: Down with man!

CAT: Miaou-yau. Death is painful!

MONKEY: I call on you to start the animal revolution!

We are chosen by God to cleanse this earth of that human filth

Which pollutes the rivers,

Burns the forests,

Soils the skies,

And stinks on earth like no other being!

Did ever a beast beat its breast in despair,

Did ever a thrush want to blush?

Did ever a deer contract gonorrhea,

Did ever a bird quail at birth?

Did ever a creature need Nietzsche to teach her?

O, Man is the shame of this earth!

VOICES: Bravo! Ra, ra, ra!

DOG: Don't listen to him. The monkey is descended from man!

PARROT: Have you read your Darwin?

CAT: I prefer Annie S. Swan.

BEAR: *climbing on to the table*] Comrades, we decree the Revolution of the Beasts!

MONKEY: Wait a minute: now the question is how? why? where?

CAT: Where? what? how?

BEAR: What? how? where? Man will be devoured!

MONKEY: But we are civilized non-human beings and cannot condone anything of the sort. We moderns, we sensitive intellectuals!

CAT: Yiau, yiau. Aue luv, aue luv.

 The sight of blood I cannot bear

 Or I get queasy.

 Please, please, settle the affair amicably.

 Bring to pass the kingdom of Beauty, Goodness and Sweetbreads!

 The resurrection of the Gazelle!

STAG: Stupid bitch!

 All or nothing at all!

 Hit hard!

 God is on our side!

 Through Sick and Sin,

 Trespassers will be prosecuted.

 A safe stronghold our God is still.

 Long live General Bear. Hip, hip, hurrah!

DOG: For reasons of public morality you are requested to adjust your clothing before leaving the building.

MONKEY: But the spirit! the spirit! The Ideal!

 A new time-reckoning begins!

 It's not a question of eating up all humans,

 But of our sacred rights as animals,

 The right to sniff at all trees, bushes, lamp-posts.

 And walls without consideration of synthetic morality,

 The right to mate in the middle of the street

 Without fear of nagging old maids,

 The right to piss on monuments, kiosks and fountains

 Even during ceremonial occasions,

 The right . . .

BEAR: Si-lence. Rub-bish—non-sense!
  I am the bear! Atten-shun!
  Revolution has nothing to do with Idealism!
  Mankind must die out—lock, stocking and barrel!
  Atten-shun! Chest out!
  Parade of the Legion!
  Jews not admitted.
  A toast to the Fatherland.
CAT: But what abaht luv—luv?
MONKEY: The Ideal! The Ideal!
  We want to establish a spiritual animal republic!
  I proclaim as programme—The New Paradise!
  Re-organization of agriculture.
  Spring to last nine months.
  Meadows to produce a juicier type of grass for the cows,
  With lots of chrysanthemum additive
  Instead of the proletarian dandelion.
  Birds to pay 10 per cent grazing rights
  Because they have all the continents to choose from.
  Daily at five o'clock humans to piss on our cereal and turnip
  crops . . .
BEAR: In three days Methusalem is dead!
  All animals in the zoo know my slogan:
  'Parting is such sorrow'
  Copyright reserved.
  Please do not spit.
  Forward March!
  I shall lead you onwards to the greatest event in animal history!
STAG: Eeh! Peace and Order!
  Hit hard!
  Right incline!
  Brutality is strength.
  The Beast is his own best friend.
  God with us.
  METHUSALEM *wakes up, blinks his eyes, smiles. All the animals
  suddenly assume their previous lifeless positions.* METHUSALEM *slides
  his hand along his right sleeve after a fly whose buzzing . . . zzzz . . .
  one can hear clearly and murmurs sleepily*] Did you wake me up,
  you little beastie?

III

Methusalem has nodded off again. The same room, but new lighting, which brings out hitherto unnoticed objects, change of lighting takes the place of change of scene. The centre window gets bigger and lets in bright blue light. The wallpaper, till now dark and worn, is now painted with red and yellow lianas and birds. Ida and Aunt Emma.

IDA: Yesterday evening he whispered to me:
  Miss, your hair has the fragrance of mignonette!
  You know what that means.

AUNT EMMA: Who, he? Stop this foolery, silly goose.
  When will you practise the C sharp major scale?
  You went wrong, all wrong the last time!

IDA: We travelled in trams with the wings of Aurora.
  It was raining stars.
  The conductor didn't want to let us pay,
  So lovely did I look.

AUNT EMMA: When will you study your English grammar?
  And the mayonnaise for the haddock!
  And father's cushion not embroidered yet!
  What will your poor, poor mother say?

IDA: The roses have a thousand mouths
  And I have but one to sing my joy:
  That made me sad the whole night through.

AUNT EMMA: Will you please answer when your aunt is speaking to you.

IDA: The birds sing green garlands
  From East to West.
  The trees sparkle
  Millions of eyes and hearts
  On trembling stalks.

AUNT EMMA: That's what comes of taking you to the theatre!
  The Censor should cut that whole Margarita episode out of 'Faust'.
  Dreaming has been your moral ruin.

IDA: Did we not pass through a great dark forest,
  And behind each lamp-post robbers crouched?
  Then he came and rescued us with his voice!

AUNT EMMA: You're feverish, my child.

But stop, on the stairs, yesterday evening didn't that Russian
student from the fifth floor say hullo?

How did you come to know him, then?

IDA: He has a voice like honey!

AUNT EMMA: I have forbidden you to talk to him.

IDA: Heaven has lent the blue of the skies to his eyes.

AUNT EMMA: A little Jew-boy like that with snotty eyelashes.

IDA: No, proud as a tree
And his brow a tower in the twilight.

I love him! I love him! Love, love, love, love.

AUNT EMMA: Iniquitous girl!
Wanton hussy!
With a student, of all things! A student!

IDA: *singing to a well-known melody*] I'm in love, I'm in love, I'm
in love, etc.

GRANDMOTHER: *bending forward out of her portrait*] So I sang at sweet
sixteen when Methusalem led me to the altar.

MAID: *coming in at the door with a tray*]
So I sang too when the Sergeant of the Guards
Roamed up and down outside our window in the evenings,
And my mother was already secretly baking the cake.
He had top-boots which cost a fortune.
And his epaulettes were a strawberry red—
And yet he left me . . .
And Mama died of a broken heart.

AUNT EMMA: *sobbing*] So I sang too when my cousin brought me
chocs,
And once when we were in the cinema together,
I sobbed and wept into my hankie,
Which he took away as a sacred relic
And . . . didn't ever come back . . .

IDA: You poor women all drying up!
Like the violets I pressed in page fifty-five of my poetry book
Lost spring times.

AUNT EMMA: *drying her tears and coming to*] That is too much!
What's to become of you!
No grammar learnt,
No mayonnaise for supper!
What will the Joneses say!

That's no match.
A Russian student, a Bolshevik!
Great God, what a calamity!
Darkness.

IV

Same room. Change of lighting: bright yellow. Arc light. The window is now wide open. A wardrobe standing pretty near the centre lights up from within and becomes the glass door of a lift. And in fact a lift can be seen stopping, the door springs open and Felix Methusalem steps out. Felix is the modern mathematical man. For a mouth he wears a copper mega-phone, for a nose he has a telephone receiver, for eyes two gold coins, for forehead and hat a typewriter, and on top he has antennae which light up every time he speaks. Every sentence he speaks is accompanied by a continuous 'Allo! Allo!'

FELIX: Allo Allo! Morning, Pahpah. Business slack on Bourse.

METHUSALEM: My God! You don't say!

FELIX: *pulls out a notebook and reads off everything. Sometimes he writes something down in it. Business voice*] Russian Leather 3¾.

METHUSALEM: My God! You don't say!

FELIX: Toreador Shoe holding its own at 62.

METHUSALEM: My God! You don't say!

FELIX: Revolution in Hawaii. Allo Allo.

METHUSALEM: My God! You don't say!

FELIX: Lady Cashier in Hamburg branch up the spout. Sick leave granted. Allo.

METHUSALEM: Damn and blast!

FELIX: Celluloid buttons up. Number ZT 23.

METHUSALEM: Confound them. My God. Call the old lady to see if the goulash is ready yet.

FELIX: Five million rubber heels sold. Allo Allo.

METHUSALEM: My son! My little Felix! A genius! The Napoleon of Box-Calf!

FELIX: Allo, Allo! Strike in our factory. Police called in. Great demonstration on now, ten o'clock. Pulls out his watch. Twenty children dead from hunger already. Allo, Allo. Filthy mob. Get them by the throat. Workers demand five-hour day at new rates. Allo, Allo.

METHUSALEM: *springs out of his armchair for the first time, runs about the room, dragging his foot bandages after him and flailing with his arms*] Jesus Christ! Mama. A strike. We are lost! Police! Murder and destruction. New rates. I am choking. Ooh, my leg. And the goulash will be getting cold. Good God, are there no laws? What a trial to be a factory owner. If I'm murdered those love letters from Anna will be found in my safe. O, what miserable wretches we are! If my grandfather could have guessed this. He always used to say: 'The people, yes the people!' Strike, why a strike? Why not 'flu? Or the yellow peril. War with Honduras for all I care. Why, why does it have to be a strike in *my* factory? The Toreador shoe just on the market too. My God, oh, my poor, good Mama! [*he stands for a moment and sniffs around*] Is there no smell of burning yet? [*meanwhile* FELIX *has calmly put away his notebook, gone to the lift, and disappeared.* METHUSALEM *flings the window open: there a screaming threatening mob can be seen approaching. Men, women with children in their arms. An omnibus is stopped and pushed up to* METHUSALEM'S *window. The* STUDENT *climbs on to the roof of the bus and begins to speak*].

STUDENT: Comrades, fellow-workers! Look at the bloated bourgeois, the blood-sucker who stuffs himself on golden brown beef steaks and succulent asparagus every day!

VOICES: Hear, hear!

STUDENT: Your children are freezing,
Your mothers have no coal for the fire,
But this Methusalem wears silk ties,
And changes his socks every day.

VOICES: Hear, hear!

STUDENT: Poor, proletariat, race of Prometheus,
Humanity flung into chains,
I will liberate you with my radial mind,
Lead you upwards to the hills and sky-scrapers of fortune,
So that all shall use the same stairway to the stars,
And no man have a jam tart more than his brother!

VOICES: Hear, hear! Never heard his like! Prophet! Hurrah!

STUDENT: But who is stopping you?
Methusalem, the lazy dog,
The man who smokes twelve-inch cigars,
Plays poker,

Has shares in the Venus Bar,
And gobbles goulash every day . . .

A great tumult ensues. The mob presses forward into Methusalem's home. From all sides a cross-fire of shouts: 'To the lamp-post/Wage structure/Potatoes/Up with Lenin/Explosion/New Rates/Beef/Child died/Capitalism/Marx/Shit/Petrol/Freedom'. As the crowd presses forward METHUSALEM *creeps out of his hide-hole, obviously trembling and upset, now with his face in his hands, now clutching at his belly. After a few hesitant steps he dares to press a button fixed near the door . . . whereupon a safe fixed on the left opens and six policemen armed with revolvers step out. The mob screams and scatters. While things are quietening down two gold-braided lackeys bring in a lavishly-carved commode, help* METHUSALEM *to unbutton his trousers and pull them down and seat him on the afore-mentioned stool. The mob is completely mastered. The policemen stand stiff and respectful.* METHUSALEM *smiles and farts. Curtain. There can be an interval here.*

V

IDA'S RENDEZVOUS WITH THE STUDENT

Park grounds, a path which divides the stage in two with split lighting. Left, the atmosphere round Ida, the girl in love, pink cloud, little flowers in grass and thin bushes, birds. Right, an old wall, grey. Lamp-post. Student atmosphere. Towards the middle, the wall has two posters: one shows a beautiful girl with snow-white teeth and the caption: 'COL-GIBBS IS BEST FOR LOVE'; the other ad. has a detective in tail-coat and mask, with caption in large letters: 'SHERLOCK HOLMES DETECTIVE AGENCY—DIVORCES GUARANTEED IN THREE MONTHS!!'

Ida is simply dressed, pink lawn blouse.

Student—there are three of him on stage, to be played by three identical masked players, they are his Ego, his Superego and his Id, which together make up one individual. To make this clear each wears the appropriate symbol in large white letters on his hat EGO, SUPEREGO, ID. Each takes a little step forward when it is his turn to speak.

EGO: That was pretty cunning, to get her to come here.

I'll show myself in public with this beautiful girl,
The Millionairess Methusalem,
Then the boys from the gym will open their eyes.
Milly the milliner will be really annoyed
That she didn't go dancing with me last night.

ID: *snooping around everywhere*] Behind that fence would be O.K.
Curse autumn: the bushes give no cover.
Still, it gets dark now pretty early.
On the other hand the lamps might well be lit.
Good old September
When all the leaves and women fall.

IDA: I danced through the streets here to see you,
The cobble-stones were rubies,
And in my heart the blue-bells were ringing.

SUPEREGO: Sweet miss, for six thousand years I've been waiting
For the tramcar to come
To reveal my heart to you!

IDA: Do you write sonnets too?

SUPEREGO: The wild woods of Romance as a present I bear you
And grazing therein are crystal white does.

EGO: They are at least cheaper than flowers from the shop.

SUPEREGO: On my lips I bear burning poems.

EGO: And an old rubber denture behind them.

SUPEREGO: Oh, bashful beloved
You
Your nose
The veins in your neck,
Your garters
Your fragrant arm-pits
Goddess mine!

EGO: Why must all loving grow so sentimental,
Poor mortals you, who only deal in dreams.
I tell you Princes fade away to phantoms,
And love's a purge to purify blood-streams.

IDA: This day is the first in my life I'm alive,
The sun's a chrysanthemum, shining for you
Your brow is a tower, a column of ivory.
From its top I can spot all the world born anew.
All places are named for you

93

All cities are built by you.
The temple-bells of Asia, the dockers of Australia
The clocks when they strike,
Strike only for you.

ID: Now, now or never!
Nobody in the park: the nannies long since gone to bed
And not yet time for the bourgeois' post-prandial stroll.
The park-keepers are tired and lazy . . .
Now fling her on the turf,
Her lips are trembling,
And black night is trickling down her spine.
Stop, curses! The ground is damp,
Her blouse will get dirty.
Oh, why didn't I bring my mac!

SUPEREGO: Your aunt is such a good person.
Are you fond of geography?
In Brazil the railway engines are painted red.
Our janitor's cat had six kittens this morning,
Six devils with sulphur eyes, they were drowned, so she said.
Then my landlady said, he is laughing, she said.
Well, what else could she have said!
Do you know Berlioz, Miss Methusalem?
He is the clarion call of our century.
That's what it said in the paper, word of honour;
Or shall we buy a second-class ticket
To wherever you want, to Mexico or Cythera:
I'll pay for everything!
I have a very good character, you know!

EGO: Am I mad? Why make her think of other things!
With two-and-six in my pocket
I should make this park conjure up primeval forest and paradise!

IDA: To you, man of men, I surrender myself
You are my destiny, miracle-maker.
You win the bull-fights in picture papers
You ride the screen with tyrannical beard, booted and spurred.
You are Goya's Adonis, hung high in the gallery,
You are the handsome blond officer
In fancy quarters opposite us.

ID: Ye Gods and little fishes! Now would have been the time.

94

Bloody bad luck, I just had to fling her down
When along comes an old dame, giving her poodle a piddle—
Ambrosian hour for ever ruined!

IDA *smiles sweetly at him, not understanding.*

EGO: And yet maybe it's better it did not happen:
She'd have been sure to notice the holes in my shirt,
The ones my landlady now refuses to mend.
She would have seen I wear false cuffs
And cufflinks not made to match.
Maybe my clap is not really gone . . .

ID: You coward, look at her bosom straining
And eager for pain in the vee of her dress.

EGO: No, no, what if she notices my halitosis from
That rotten tooth I haven't had filled!

ID *lunges at* EGO *and deals out a few boots and cuffs.* EGO *howls loudly and rolls on the grass.* ID *tears at his hair and arranges his tie. Meanwhile* SUPEREGO *is busily occupied with* IDA.

SUPEREGO: Sweet Miss, when shall we go to the Symphony Concert together?
Beethoven's Ninth will dry-clean your soul.
I know lots of painters with beards and floppy ties.
We shall drink Russian tea in their studios,
From my roof-top you can see three hundred chimney pots
Like a forest in autumn, and far off the canal,
With ships from India, bearing the world in their holds.

IDA: Happily we shall sit and eat ices on terraces!
We shall hear the first bird at five
Fall out of his sleep and into our lives!
You are the pilot flying off through the sunset!
The heavenly rider, the Derby winner!

EGO: Silly goose, I'm sick of poetry!
I haven't had her, so what's the point of more idolatry.
Besides, her cotton gloves smell of sweat,
And sentimentality is anaemic yet.
Oh, give me the pro from the Buffalo Bar,
Bursting with rosy vulgarity,
And gleaming garter shining through her dress.

ID: Yes, leave the milk-coffee saturated middle-class maiden,
Let her breasts wither in her brassières,

A sweet little violet soon to be stuck
Between the covers of the family albums.
Let some uncouth young executive type
Prick his fingers on her corsets.

EGO: But she is supposed to come into five millions.

SUPEREGO: Beloved, will you permit me to send you a picture post-card?

ID: Take her, there's still time, there's nobody coming!
And if there's a kid, the old man'll have to fork out.

EGO: When the Red Revolution comes
I'll come into the money anyway!

IDA: The trees are coming adrift,
Birds nibble away at the moon
And we too, we too, my Faust, my Lohengrin, my Pope!

SUPEREGO: You mustn't catch cold here!
You must go home and drink up your peppermint tea!
Au revoir, Calliope, my star!

EGO: I'll get you yet: in my room tomorrow!

ID: Stupid BIRD!
Curtain.

VI

The Methusalems have visitors. Three couples are led in almost simul-
taneously by servants. They all know each other and, talking loudly,
immediately begin to examine all the objects in the room, handle them, etc.
The men, all wear identical ready-made suits. Their face-masks express
Greed, Envy, Curiosity. From time to time they inspect things through
opera-glasses. The middle-class ladies are wearing extraordinary models as
hats, genuine geranium pots, stuffed birds, or cardboard government
buildings in miniature, zebra and buffalo hides, dresses either with very
long trains or with skirts above the knees. The are the Enteritises, the
Bellés and Kingdumbcombes.

MR. ENTERITIS: How d'ye do.
MR. BELLÉ: How d'ye do.
MR. KINGDUMBCOMBE: How d'ye do.
MRS. ENTERITIS: How low the rooms are!

MRS. BELLÉ: And no ventilation. It's quite stifling.

MRS. KINGDUMBCOMBE: And my dear, the dust. It's really an impertinence to invite us here.

MR. ENTERITIS: Terrible weather to-day.

MR. BELLÉ: Yes, if it would only rain at least!

MR. KINGDUMBCOMBE: What? Rain? Are you mad? My shoes have just been soled.

MRS. KINGDUMBCOMBE: O, does anybody know of a good laxative?

MR. ENTERITIS: *to* MR. BELLÉ] Now listen: first you buy a body belt.

MRS. ENTERITIS: *sticking her oar in*] No, first take some cold Kruschen salts and boil them in water . . .

MR. ENTERITIS: If there's no gas get the plumber in.

MRS. ENTERITIS: Then you have to wash your feet.

MR. ENTERITIS: And remember, no tips.

MR. BELLÉ: That's all very well, but what about the boil on my neck. You haven't said what I have to do about that!

MRS. BELLÉ: But don't you see, hubby, they are not telling you on purpose. They'd see you dead first.

MRS. KINGDUMBCOMBE: Put Italian mustard on the spot. Don't you get any exercise?

MR. ENTERITIS: Sure, we go fishing together every year in the canal.

MRS. KINGDUMBCOMBE: Reading newspapers is very unhealthy. The stop-press columns are very bad for sleep.

MRS. BELLÉ: Incidentally, did you hear about the latest little murder? A son, who stuck a genuine silver fork into his grandmother's heart, to kill her. Shakespeare has nothing so fantastic. Imagine a fork with four sharp points. How the blood must have spurted out!

MRS. ENTERITIS: And cauliflower has gone up a lot.

METHUSALEM: *coming in*] My dear friends! How hard life is! [*Sits down*].

MRS. KINGDUMBCOMBE: The end of the world.

MRS. BELLÉ: It is, nowadays!

MR. KINGDUMBCOMBE: In the meantime I think.

METHUSALEM: Well, what do you think?

MRS. BELLÉ: Listen, Bellé, Mr. Kingdumbcombe thinks something!

MR. ENTERITIS: Splendid, phenomenal.

MR. KINGDUMBCOMBE: Yes, well, what I think is this, you see . . . it's like this, I . . . don't really think anything.

MR. BELLÉ: That really is the end!

METHUSALEM: Oh, how dear life is!

MR. ENTERITIS: Life is dear.

MRS. ENTERITIS: Dear is what life is.

MR. BELLÉ: We're starving to death.

MRS. KINGDUMBCOMBE: There's no foie in the pâté.

MR. BELLÉ: What a government!

MR. ENTERITIS: What? You dare utter a word against democracy and you'll have me to deal with.

MR. BELLÉ: But quite the contrary. I'm a Socialist, Royalist, that is, a member of the Independent People's Party, do you see?

MR. KINGDUMBCOMBE: All the same, I think . . .

MRS. ENTERITIS: What an extremely interesting afternoon.

METHUSALEM: My son has just bought himself a blue check tie.

MR. ENTERITIS: Our daughter is studying shorthand now.

METHUSALEM: My son has invented a new slipper.

MRS. ENTERITIS: Our daughter subscribes to the Catholic Library.

METHUSALEM: My Felix is a member of the Geniuses' Club.

MRS. ENTERITIS: And my daughter Irma is learning Spinoza by heart. Isn't she, dear? How wonderful, why don't we marry the two of them off?

METHUSALEM: Tip-top idea! And when shall the wedding be?

MR. ENTERITIS *pulls a large wall calendar out of his pocket. Meanwhile* AMALIA *comes in all dolled-up, hair-do, powdered, pearl diadem on her head, and a filthy kitchen apron round her middle. She carries in the whole tea-set herself.*

AMALIA: Oh, my dear guests. So nice of you to come. There is so much to be done. Please excuse me. It's so difficult with maids. It's all very well for them to talk. But do you know what my Sieglinde did to our genuine antique Dresden porcelain chamber pot, an heirloom from Uncle Hugo now passed away, who was Corporal in the 4th Company of the Foot Artillery and just imagine, he smoked nothing but black tobacco! He gave me his picture just before his trip to Holland, you have to understand that nobody in our family has ever had rheumatism, we're very healthy stock. Well now, this Uncle Hugo, whose brother met a Customs Man in the middle of the street on New Year's Eve, 1900, died one day. And we were just in the middle of the

monthly wash and it began to pour . . . then he said . . . he said
. . . well, what did I want to say, Methusalem, do help me.
*The guests have stopped listening some time ago, some have fallen
asleep, others catch flies, etc.*

MRS. ENTERITIS: *continuing the discussion with* METHUSALEM] No, the
marriage can only take place if we have the invitations printed on
genuine parchment.

METHUSALEM: Genuine parchment! But consider what an expense
that means. Wouldn't an extra paragraph in the paper do just as
well?

MRS. ENTERITIS: You want to save money at the expense of our
children?

MR. ENTERITIS: The Methusalem family must be very mean.

METHUSALEM: Meanness maketh money.

MRS ENTERITIS: Our Irma would rather take the veil. No parchment.
Come, hubby, I don't wish to sojourn longer within these walls.

MR. ENTERITIS: Mr. Methusalem, I am sorry, But besides you were
already a bankrupt in 1898. Pshaw. A chip off the old block like
your son will be. No parchment. Never heard the like! [*He takes
his wife by the arm and departs noisily with her*].

AMALIA: *carries on serving the tea*] And if you knew what the cook I
once had used to put on her head. Black Brazilian straw and
three fat cherries on it. Two-and-six—a song—only cooks have
that kind of luck. And the baker's wife goes dancing at the
Tivoli every Sunday and she has a young cousin who wanted to
become an architect, but we know what conditions are like in
Europe, don't we . . .

MRS. KINGDUMBCOMBE: *prods her husband in the ribs*] Well, go on,
say it, Kingdumbcombe.

MR. KINGDUMBCOMBE: Yes, well, I just wanted to say we have a son
too.

MRS. KINGDUMBCOMBE: *to* AMALIA] Your tea is a miracle.

AMALIA: That's because I made it. Just imagine, the cook always
put in four spoons instead of three. And it is imported direct
from Ceylon . . . the best brand, of course, you know the price.

MRS. KINGDUMBCOMBE: You know, our son wears a panama.

AMALIA: Our Ida has a perm every week.

MRS. KINGDUMBCOMBE: We saw her yesterday in the main street.

AMALIA: Oh, how nice of you!

MRS. KINGDUMBCOMBE: Do you know Einstein?

AMALIA: The dentist?

MRS. KINGDUMBCOMBE: My son was up in the mountains at Whitsun and he sent him a postcard. All his friends put their names to it—Fritz Maier, who has a bad eye, that is, it's not so bad since he put a plum poultice on it, and . . .

AMALIA: *sighing*] Yes, yes, our Ida.

MRS. KINGDUMBCOMBE: Our Maxie.

METHUSALEM: My Ida! When she plays the Moonlight Sonata on the piano, I'm telling you . . .

MR. KINGDUMBCOMBE: They must marry!

AMALIA: On one condition—they must take out a subscription to Her Majesty's Theatre.

MR. KINGDUMBCOMBE: *climbs on the table*] My dear friends, I hereby solemnly announce [*sobs loudly into his handkerchief*] the engagement of our two children, on the one hand Max, and on the other hand [*bends downs to whisper to his wife*] have you looked into his bank account? [*he sobs*] But what I was going to say—yes, what I really intended to say . . . !

Great emotion among the guests, who shake hands, embrace and all burst out crying. The room grows dark a moment, during which time the guests and all traces of the visit disappear.

VII

The same room. Darker lighting, which later turns pinker when Ida appears. Methusalem and Amalia alone.

METHUSALEM: *rubbing his hands*] Another good bit of business.

AMALIA: The Kingdumbcombes have a seven-roomed flat.

METHUSALEM: The Detective Agency I put on them have just sent in a report: They are in tripe in a big way.

AMALIA: A first-floor flat. Unexpectedly good match.

METHUSALEM: Magnificent prospects for next war. I go into partnership with my son-in-law—Central Cattle Trust Incorporated. We buy up all the cattle in Europe: the hides for our shoe factory, the tripes for army sausages, the meat can be sold as a waste product.

AMALIA: What does Max really look like? The Crown Prince?

METHUSALEM: I believe he has red hair. When I last saw him five years ago he was parting his hair on the left.

AMALIA: *goes to the door right and coos*] Ida, Ida! My little turtle dove! Little water-lily! Little canary bird! My daughter, where are you!

IDA: *comes floating in, dreamily, hair streaming loosely*]
The trees are floating for joy, like
Airships whose cables
Autumn has cast off.
Birds sit in them
As in the dining-car
For Cairo
And my heart is among them.

METHUSALEM: Have you heard the latest?

IDA: A pink star trembles in my body.
The wolves howled in the wind this night,
But angels with cotton-wool wings
Came and comforted me saying
'Your child will have eyes of jade.'

AMALIA: Completely screwy.

METHUSALEM: Read too much Zola.

AMALIA: You had the educating of her.

IDA: *with pathos*] You transported me nigh unto death from ecstasy!!!

METHUSALEM: The girl is playing the Virgin Mary.
Too much Catechism probably.

AMALIA: You had the educating of her.

METHUSALEM: Are you not ashamed of yourself before your old father?

IDA: In the museum I've seen embryos!
Wizened old men in green alcohol
Smiling of birth and of death
Pain of becoming
Or perhaps of the already having been?

METHUSALEM: *wild with rage, screaming*] You prostitute!

AMALIA: No, listen my child, be reasonable!
You see, from to-day, you are betrothed.

IDA: Betrothed! Oh yes, to an oriental prince,
On fiery chariots of Luna Park

We conquered purple Orion.

We touched Saturn with our naked finger

Then he swore an oath that he would marry me,

Probably the day after to-morrow!

AMALIA: My child, you must take a little camomile tea.

IDA: He comes from Baku and is studying medicine.

His home country is nothing but one great forest of acacias.

METHUSALEM: You're driving us to the grave, to the damp, dark family vault!

You whore, you prostitute!

IDA: A child is just a drop fallen from God, he said,

And then he said, read Schopenhauer.

AMALIA: Oh, God, what will the Kingdumbcombes say?

METHUSALEM: I'll teach you respect.

AMALIA: I'll fetch you a glass of raspberry syrup. [*Off, weeping noisily. At the same time* FELIX *appears in his lift, equipped exactly as in IV*].

FELIX: *looks round, his phone rings, the antennae on his head spark*]

Allo, Allo! There's something wrong here.

METHUSALEM: Methusalem and Co. is lost.

FELIX: Allo, Allo! Have the meat tariffs gone down?

Are ladies' stockings unsteady?

Is there a tax on yellow kid gloves?

Has the Heart-Credit Bank burst?

METHUSALEM: Worse! Worse even than that!

FELIX: Our competitor has been elected to Parliament?

Not a single striker died yesterday?

Our agent in Hong Kong has the nose-bleed again?

Allo, Allo, Allo, what has happened?

METHUSALEM: Your sister Ida 'knows' a man.

FELIX: *staggering back a step, with pathos*] Im-possible!

IDA: Yes, dear brother, you man of great understanding.

You who know when the sun sets in Ostend,

You who daily intone the cotton prices like a prayer you have learned by rote,

You who, a benefactor to men, cannot see them running around bare-foot:

Understand my startled little heart

Which soon must beat for two.

FELIX: This is the giddy limit, isn't it, Allo?

METHUSALEM: She is making fun of you too.

FELIX: You a Methusalem through and through,
You dishonour our holy name, our sacred firm!
The honour of the Box-Calf Trust is at stake.
Our customers will be horrified and doubt our advertising.
The new Toreador shoe won't sell!
Oh, what misfortune assails us, Ida!

METHUSALEM: A child! She has a child and even dares to confess it to her old father, that is the limit! Have you not an ounce of morality in your body?

IDA: I have a baby in my body, pink and pure.

METHUSALEM: We must do something about public opinion. Announce a big Sale.

FELIX: 20 per cent reductions.

METHUSALEM: Ooh, my leg, fallen whore of a daughter!

FELIX: *walks excitedly up and down the stage*] My honour, my honour assailed!
O, how I suffer! Allo, Allo, Allo! I have it!
I shall shoot the fellow down!
He pulls out a revolver, sparks on all antennae, rings, makes 'Allo, Allo', and climbs into the lift going down. Off.
AMALIA *comes back with a glass of syrup. She sees* METHUSALEM *and* IDA *weeping loudly.*

AMALIA: Yes, but basically, I still don't understand a word of the affair.
Tell me, child, what has really happened?
Did a man in the street nod to my little Ida?
Or has Idey Widey received a p.c. from a man?
Or what, what terrible thing can have happened then?

IDA: *approaches her tenderly and embraces her*] Mother, in my womb, a little pink babe.
AMALIA *utters a cry of pain, but quickly places the glass she is carrying on the table, after carefully wiping the foot of the glass with her dress, not to dirty anything—only then does she collapse and groan.*

AMALIA: Merciful heavens, I believe I'm going to faint.
Curtain.

VIII

Venue of the duel. Early morning. Park grounds. A lamp-post. Felix, this time in morning coat, hair oiled down and monocle. The Student.

FELIX: So you seduced my sister.

STUDENT: And what if I did.

FELIX: Insulted my family.

STUDENT: So?

FELIX: That calls for revenge.

STUDENT: Pooh, pooh, pooh.

FELIX: Mean cur!

STUDENT: Are you serious?
  Now, look, what has really happened?
  Your sister is in love with me:
  What can one do against the sexual urge?
  Any seduction means it's what the person really wants.
  What you call it is unimportant.
  What else has happened? A little spermatozoon—
  That's better than the 'flu virus any day.

FELIX: Allo! I call upon God to witness . . .

STUDENT: You must not squabble with God.
  In His eyes there is no crime and no nakedness.
  'Everything human is by definition profound'. (Goethe).

FELIX: Sir, you annoy me!

At the back of the stage the following picture is presented scenically or by film. A funeral, grotesque and comical: the horses with tall palm fronds on their heads. On the coffin lies a coffee-grinder. Bishops in full regalia stagger along behind it. The choir-boys in red gowns eat sandwiches. Large and comical crowd. Directly behind the hearse the mourners: the brother and the limping sister of the dead lady, with the following dialogue:

SISTER: But she was always so mean!

BROTHER: Don't shout so loud, my boss is just passing.

SISTER: Last time we were at her place, she said somebody had said I said she used to eat horse-meat.

BROTHER: Well, she won't have that expense any more.

SISTER: You know, those earrings of hers that come to me are worked in genuine platinum.

BROTHER: What? They come to me!

SISTER: She promised them to me!

BROTHER: She wanted to give them to my wife five years ago!

SISTER: *stamps and shouts*] Jewellery comes to the female heirs!

BROTHER: Just quote me chapter and verse to prove it.

SISTER: You dog! Marie was meanness incarnate. [*she flings herself on the coffin and tears off the pall*] I'm betrayed. What a filthy trick!

BISHOP: *behind them both*] DO-MI-NUS vo-bis-cum!

The Vision disappears.

FELIX: And my sister was still a virgin.

STUDENT: And why not, pray?
Isn't every man entitled to deflower at least once in his life?
Up till then I had slept with 137 non-virgins,
And I wanted to have an original, so to speak.

FELIX: Yes, but my sister!

STUDENT: Your personal misfortune.

FELIX: You are a Bolshie and wear false cuffs!

STUDENT: And my shoes are down-at-heel.

FELIX: You are a swine!

STUDENT: I have holes in my shirt.

FELIX: Not a pennyworth of honour in your body!

STUDENT: Where do you buy honour? Can you get it on the rations?

FELIX: You must die by your own hand. Surely you would not make me a murderer?

STUDENT: And do you think me a nice fellow, who will spare you the necessity?

FELIX: You swine, you Jew, you enemy of the people, you jackal, you mangy cur [*groping for words*] you, you dung-heap, you syph sore, you, you . . .

STUDENT: *hands in his pockets, laughs*] Mr. Methusalem, your fly's undone! [FELIX *turns away quickly, bends over, fumbles at the appropriate place. New Vision in the background: a wedding; grotesque peasant style: the groom in top-hat and peasant smock, the bride all in white except for a black mourning veil round her head, the guests stagger along behind them; three musicians marching on in front, flute, fiddle and drums, playing 'The Lorelei'. Dialogue between the bride and groom.*

GROOM: What a miserable wedding-present—an old bath-tub.

BRIDE: You're just saying that because it comes from my aunt. You find fault with my whole family.

GROOM: *laughing*] A bath-tub!

BRIDE: You've drunk too much champagne.

GROOM: Oh, so you are bringing that up against me already.

BRIDE: It's going to be some life with a man like you!

GROOM: If only I had never married you!

BRIDE: Did you notice my mother's velvet hat. She kept it specially from my Confirmation.

GROOM: It looks like it.

BRIDE: Are we leaving direct for Venice tonight, lammikin?

GROOM: In the first place I'm no lammikin. In the second place we spend the night here. In the third place we're only going to Blackpool.

BRIDE: *runs back to the guests in tears*] Mummy, mummy, Oskar's being nasty to me already.

MOTHER: How dare you! My good Scripture Union daughter!

A fight breaks out. Umbrellas and walking-sticks flail. The band plays a funeral march. All disappear in the wings.

FELIX: *thoughtfully*] But in all you seem to have some character.
You could make a first-rate business-man!
So if the aforementioned baby were to have the absolute cheek
To insist on seeing the light of day,
I offer you a Directorship
In our Jamaica venture
On one condition: never return to Europe!

STUDENT: *with pathos*] What point in travelling to Jamaica!
One can never escape oneself!
Even below the equator you still remain a Methusalem
And I the father of your nephew.
Believe me, even at the North Pole life is a bore
And if you eat too many sardines, you'll belch.

FELIX: *momentarily forsaking his part*] Did you study philosophy?

STUDENT: The stupidity of mankind is so great
That anybody who says so is immediately hailed as a genius.

FELIX: *remembering himself*] So you were trying to insult me?

STUDENT: Only the truth can wound.

FELIX: *pulls out the revolver*] Then I'm sorry, this is going to hurt me more than it hurts you, but . . .

He shoots. The STUDENT *immediately falls to the ground. He visibly breathes out his soul, which leaves him in the shape of an overcoat, and floats upwards. Thereupon the* STUDENT *stands up again.*

STUDENT: Behold my departing soul! Say hello to your sister for me, will you?

He raises his hat and departs.

Curtain.

IX

At Methusalem's home. New, golden lighting. From different sides, Veronica and the Student appear simultaneously.

STUDENT: *makes gestures significant of highest intimacy to the apparently unapproachable lady*] You here, loveliest of ladies?

VERONICA: Sir, I know you not.

STUDENT: All the more reason to make up for it.

VERONICA: But I am betrothed to Mr. Methusalem.

STUDENT: Oh, how lonely I am!

VERONICA: Don't make fun of other people!

STUDENT: We shall never, never meet!

VERONICA: Do you want me to burst into tears?

STUDENT: You can't be horizontal if you want to see the horizon.

VERONICA: No insults, please!

STUDENT: But my name is Robert!

VERONICA: Oh well, in that case! [*she proffers her rouged cheek and he kisses it very loudly*].

STUDENT: Oh, how I love . . . a bit of cottage pie.

MAN IN THE AUDIENCE: Hahahaha! [*laughs out loud*].

STUDENT: Don't laugh, sir, that was serious.

MAN IN THE AUDIENCE: That's really going too far. I shall lodge a complaint, ask for my money back. He's not even being funny. [*leaves with great disturbance*].

VERONICA: The swallows are auctioning spring.

STUDENT: Yesterday in the tram I met a person who said to me: 'Young man, you should never go out without an umbrella!'

VERONICA: My neckline is not nearly low enough! [*she opens it a little as she says so*].

STUDENT: Madame, you really should go skiing.

VERONICA: How about coming with me?

STUDENT: First we must murder Methusalem. That would be a good reason for taking such a big trip. Here he is, I'll come back armed.

He climbs out of the window, METHUSALEM *appears, freshly shaven, a poppy in his button-hole. Smiling.*

VERONICA: Ah, here you are at last, my little golden beetle! What's the dollar doing on the money market?

METHUSALEM: *approaches and immediately puts his hand down her bra*] Box-Calf leather is going up.

VERONICA: I'm so unhappy. I need an aeroplane.

METHUSALEM: Haven't you been deceiving me?

VERONICA: Since yesterday nobody has even looked me in the eyes!

METHUSALEM: What about the legs? *He opens her blouse all the way down*].

VERONICA: I'm so fearfully tensed up! I need a million.

METHUSALEM: Impossible. I never give away less than three million.

VERONICA: Is that so? My little student was much more gallant.

METHUSALEM: Wretched woman! You do not know how jealous I can be!

VERONICA: Then come with me to Tokyo!

METHUSALEM: Alright, but I have to wash my feet first . . .

STUDENT: *climbs in the window again and opens it wide*] Spare yourself the trouble of the journey, love, jealousy, buying flowers, washing feet and cracking jokes—I'm taking your place. Give me your wallet. In exchange I'll put you to sleep for ever.

METHUSALEM: *screams*] Murder! Thieves! Murd . . . [*thinks it over*] But, my young man, you seem to have talent. Wouldn't you rather join my firm as a salesman?

STUDENT: Your money! money! money!

METHUSALEM: Won't you consider it? I have good connections. You might be an Under-Secretary for Public Ill-fare.

STUDENT: Your money! money! money!

METHUSALEM: He really has talent.

Nothing is as solid as lovely money.

He is of my race.

For money you can buy jokes, love, spring and revolutions.

STUDENT *puts his hand in* METHUSALEM'S *coat pocket and pulls out bundles of notes.* METHUSALEM *is not able to stop him.* VERONICA *has run away in fright, furiously buttoning up her blouse again.*

STUDENT: I am the deed!

I am the Revolt, the spirit, the salt,
That will decompose your stagnant waters,
All your mouldering civilizations!
Consume in fire all your laws like old newspaper,
Knock the false dentures out of your morals,
And as for your fat bourgeois bellies . . .
He runs to the window.

METHUSALEM: Don't waste your time, my student dreamer,
Ruined wreckage of the garrets,
Revolutionary of the empty belly,
Filled with pipe dreams from cheap tobacco;
I'll take you on . . .

METHUSALEM is about to press a button. The STUDENT stops him by pulling a gun on him and simultaneously uttering a piercing whistle. Immediately there appears in the window the same mob as in IV, this time with red flags, revolutionary slogans and insignia and pictures of revolutionary leaders on long poles.

VOICES: Down with Methusalem!
String him up by his tie!
Up with Lenin!
Boiled spuds—Common Market—Freedom—Up the
Red Dean—Ten kiddies dead—Down with the
Money Moloch—Down! Down! Down!

The STUDENT tries to hurry to the window-sill to make a speech. In that second, however, METHUSALEM tears him back with all his force, stands at the window himself and begins to speak.

METHUSALEM: Comrades!

VOICES: Boo—boo—mangy dog! Tyrant!

METHUSALEM: Do I look like a tyrant!

VOICE: Not when we see your old woman, you don't.

METHUSALEM: I know your suffering. It is my suffering.

VOICE: No sympathy, please!

METHUSALEM: I am poorer than all of you together.

VOICES: How do you work that out?

METHUSALEM: Do you know what a shoe factory means?

VOICE: It means you have plenty of boots to kick workers to death with.

METHUSALEM: I started in quite a small way.
I collected cigar butts for my father outside Parisian cafés,

In Chicago I rolled petrol drums around the docks,
My own hide was tanned before I took to tanning box-calf.
And Liebknecht, did any of you know him like I did?
We lived right opposite him and saw him across the street every
day.
I'm shortly going to publish his unpublished post-cards;
He used to give half a dollar to all the street girls
So they could afford to do one less customer.

VOICE: Your bints cost half that!

METHUSALEM: Liebknecht always wore Toreador shoes!
Comrades, your very own victorious brand!
Now we'll put the new Liebknecht brand on the market
With polished points in genuine cardboard!
We'll really do business and get rich;
Come back to the factory! Strike no more!
Your work benches will be padded with red velvet,
And your machines enamelled in ruddiest red . . .

VOICES: Rubbish.
No sentimentality.
Perish.
Shit-pot.
Hang him!
Up the bourgeois.
We want bread.

METHUSALEM: Well, then, what more do you want of me?
Do you want to sleep in my bed?
Step right in! What about a drop of fine old brandy?
Or this tie? [*strips off his tie*]
Who wants my genuine camel-hair slippers? [*takes them off*]
Here. [*points round the walls*] This is a genuine Corot.
This a Kokoschka!
This sofa is early Victorian.
This tooth-glass pure rock crystal.
Genuine beet-sugar reposes in this porcelain bowl.

*During his triumphant speech a more and more threatening murmur
becomes noticeable. The mob presses forward darkly, bursts the window,
sings the 'Internationale'. But at the head of them all the* STUDENT,
holding a revolver, shoots. METHUSALEM *falls massively to the ground.
Dead. The mob comes to a halt. Flows backwards. Somebody or other*

has put a coin in the JOKE BOX *in the corner. It clatters forward with little steps, takes up position before the corpse and recites:*

JOKE BOX: Miko wants to go riding! 'Janosch,' Mikosch called to his servant one day, 'Me want go riding—you go see if barometer has fallen.' Janosch goes and comes back quickly: 'Barometer not fallen sir, still hanging firmly on nail.'

While JOKE BOX *speaks all present have scattered. The corpse of* METHUSALEM *lies alone in the front of the stage. After the joke there is the uncanny sound of a distant guffaw, the way* METHUSALEM *used to laugh.*

JOKE BOX: Janosch has broken a mirror and his master calls him to account. 'Me not have done,' pleads Janosch: 'Bassama Teremtete, me have witness who see it,' says Mikosch. Then Janosch replies: 'And me have thirty witnesses who not see it!'

Before this joke is finished FELIX *appears, as usual in his lift, his notebook and fountain-pen already poised in his hand, and speaks.*

FELIX: Allo, Allo. Order for Bucharest. Seventy-five pairs Toreador; three thousand pairs new Liebknecht brand! [*when there is no answer he only then notices the corpse at his feet*] Allo, Allo, Papa! Business is great. Come on, get up.

AMALIA: *comes in with steaming bowl*] Here is the goulash, the good old goulash. Don't let it get cold now. [*shouting*] Goodness gracious, you always let everything get cold. It's enough to make a person stop trying.

FELIX: *who has bowed his head, reverently*] I believe we are about to come into some money!

AMALIA: *also with bowed head*] Come on, now, hubby. Are you trying to annoy me, as usual? What about the goulash? [*she weeps*] You can't just die off this very moment. What will the Enteritises say. They've invited us for tomorrow.

FELIX: I must remember to buy a black tie.

AMALIA: Have you done your weeping?

FELIX: Allo, Allo, only hope the lawyer's at home.

AMALIA: What kind of funeral do you think? First, second, third class? What do you think? Third class? Don't go indulging in any unnecessary expense, do you hear? Children are always so extravagant.

FELIX *off.* AMALIA *still shouting after him as he goes.*

X

Bench in a public park. The Student and Ida with a child in her arms.
Very poor. Cast out.

IDA: It's peed on my dress again.

STUDENT: Did you buy the frankfurts?

IDA: The man in the office said I had such bucolic hips!

STUDENT: Was that worth an advance?

IDA: I should like to go to Japan.

STUDENT: My collar stud's broken again. [*the child howls*].

IDA: Our little Godfrey must become an Insurance Agent;
   He will part his hair in the middle and wear a tartan tie,
   Then he will get on in the world,
   And travel on the underground with the best of them.
   Maybe he'll be a Director of a canning factory.
   Who can tell?

STUDENT: O God, isn't life dull!

IDA: When will the Revolution be finished?

STUDENT: When the others don't have a mansion left.

IDA: And when we have one?

STUDENT: The new Revolution starts.

IDA: Why do even the stars tremble at night!

STUDENT: Keep forgetting that raincoat.

IDA: If only Godfrey would stop peeing!

STUDENT: I must buy an evening paper. [*gets up tiredly*].

METHUSALEM: *comes past them slowly from the depths of the stage*]
   Well, children, is it going to be rain? All the better. We are
   just putting a new rubber heel on the market, the Einstein. The
   hit of the autumn season. Filthy weather, thank goodness. But I
   must be off now to my goulash . . .
   Curtain.

THE WOLVES

by Alfred Brust

A Winter Play

1921

Translated by J. M. Ritchie

There appear:

TOLKENING, clergyman
ANITA, his wife
DR. JOHN JOY, medical practitioner
MISS AGATHA JOY, his sister
TORKEL

The action takes place in East Prussia

Very slow and brooding tempo

Tolkening's living-room. A little stark but not unfriendly. On the right there are two doors, on the left one. Well forward, so that on the remaining part of the wall there is room for a large, broad stove with a long broad fireside seat in front of it. Table and chairs. A gun hangs between door and stove. Between the two doors of the opposite wall is a large stag's head with antlers (or a picture of a large stag). Under it stands a grand piano. In the background a step leads into the full breadth of a semicircular bay-window area with many tall windows. The view looks out over an open landscape deep in snow. The large french window, which opens out into it, is locked. Sun-set.

On the table, spread with a cold supper, stand a samovar, a decanter and tea and liqueur glasses.

TOLKENING: *a slim man of medium height, of about 35, enters from the right through the door front. He is of simple and noble appearance. He walks into the middle of the room, his eyes transfixed, stops and struggles desperately to remember something. He seizes his skull with both hands, and lets them sink again hopelessly. He shakes his head, as if he must hurl something out of it. He catches sight of the laid table]* The Joys! Of course! Why didn't I think of that before . . . *[he goes up to the door by the stove. He tries to open it. It is locked]* — — — Anita!?

ANITA: *answers slowly from the other room]* What . . . is it? Alright— I'm—coming.

TOLKENING *affects to be puzzled over the locked door, then gives up and goes back into the room.*

ANITA *comes in. An arresting and well-built woman.*

TOLKENING: *gives a start]* Strange—the way you come into the room.

ANITA *finds this sentence incomprehensible and stands still.*

TOLKENING: I've just had a dream. And this dream—I've forgotten it. It must have been a fearful dream.

ANITA: *disconcerted]* You are always going on about your dreams! *[she takes a few heavy steps].*

TOLKENING: It is quite strange. I can't get over it. It must have been a horrible dream. All I know is, it was quite frightful! Somehow —the movement I'm making now, terrifies me to my innermost being, because somehow it reminds me of—of the dream. *[he stares fixedly].*

ANITA: *stretches lightly, runs her hands over her body, as if trying to remove words distasteful to her from her flesh]* Your Doctor Joy and his little sister are taking their time.

TOLKENING: It's been a strenuous journey. All very new and very trying . . . How do you like him, my old school friend?

ANITA: *looks away]* It's a depressing feeling, having to share this house with strange people in future.

TOLKENING: *gives her a searching look]* Strange—people?! But . . . You agreed with the whole idea of sharing the house. And as the clergyman, you know, I couldn't but be pleased, to get a sound doctor to come to our village. There was nowhere else for him to live. And you should be pleased that I've managed to attract a dear friend and his charming sister to this place. This young lady is sure to become a faithful friend for you . . . I've—known her—since her teens. And once I—even—wrote a poem about her. It turned up again recently among my papers. It isn't at all bad either—though I say it myself. I'll let you read it later if you like.

ANITA: *ignores this*] Oh well. They're here. We'll just have to get used to the idea.

TOLKENING: *with a sharp look*] He doesn't look like you'd hoped . . .

ANITA *about to protest.*

TOLKENING: No. No. Don't. I too must confess that he's terribly changed. There's something new about him I don't know yet. He's a doctor. And as such—it seems to me—he looks—right through people. That's probably all. I look—through people too, it's true. But I focus on the soul. He focuses on the body. I think —we might complement each other. Because doctors know nothing of the Gods—and clergymen know nothing of the— devils . . . Yes — — —

ANITA *takes a few more heavy steps.*

TOLKENING: *strangely startled*] The way you walk! Strange how it startles me so. [*racking his brains*] It seems somehow familiar or something. Why are the big dreams shrouded in such veils. . . .

ANITA: *ill at ease, forces a laugh*] If everybody was as afraid of their dreams as you are—my God—the poor wretches would die of terror one by one. As a priest—you should—hm— — — I think Dr. Joy is going to make an appearance at last.

A knock.

TOLKENING: Yes! It's him! Who else could be knocking! Come in! Come in! Ha ha ha ha!

ANITA *breathes a sigh of relief.*

TORKEL *opens the door carefully, glances round and then slips in quickly. His splendid build and rude good health are positively offensive. Strong, coarse, ruthless. Cleanly if eccentrically dressed.*

ANITA *taken aback, controls herself.*

TOLKENING: Mr. — — — Torkel! Good day, my dear fellow! You here on a Sunday! I hope there hasn't been a serious accident or something, you never come to see me for any other reason.

TORKEL: O—Reverend! Why would there be an accident! It's the what's-its, you know! I've brought another dozen.

TOLKENING: Twelve — — —?

ANITA: *quickly*] I asked the man to get me a few rabbits. No doubt that's what it's all about.

TORKEL: That's for sure . . . that's what it's about. That's the truth.

TOLKENING: Oh, I see . . . But — — but — hm.

TORKEL: And I just wanted to say that there's definitely no more. Nowhere. Definitely no more—see.

ANITA: *breathing heavily*] There's no longer—need for any.

TORKEL: Well, then—that's fine. I'm a Christian too, you know. Anyway it's going on for— — —

ANITA: And you want your money now . . .

TOLKENING: How much do you have coming to you?

TORKEL: Still 200 Marks, Reverend.

TOLKENING: Two— —!! Yes—I see . . . Wait, will you . . . I'll just go and fetch the money. [*he goes quickly, but unsteadily, to the room he came out of earlier*].

ANITA: You!! You!! I find it disgraceful! Do you hear me? Quite disgraceful!

TORKEL: But . . . but . . . lovely, lovely lady . . . What am I supposed to do! Lovely, lovely lady!—I, Torkel, am a man, do you understand me. And as good as the beasts any time, any time. Hm! Lovely, lovely lady . . . [*hard up against her*] I can tell you. I have *always, always, always* got some!! But . . . Hm . . . The price—you know what that is, lovely lady . . . Money? What do I want with money?! If you want! Hm!! Any time! Any time!! Yes. And nobody would ever know. I'll be waiting at the boat-shed down by the lake, when it begins to get dark.

ANITA *has slowly retreated and crumpled inwardly.*

TORKEL: We went to the village school together, Anita—you mustn't forget that. Hihihi! Can you remember? Torkel—Torkel—what a boy! And the woods—the dark woods! Hm . . . You forget your good deeds, your bad ones you *never* forget, Anita. You know—take away— — and then bring back. That's what Torkel is good at . . .

TOLKENING: *comes in*] Now then . . . here . . . here you have two hundred and *twenty* Marks. You happy now?

TORKEL: All well and good—hm . . . [*he takes the money, looks at it, hands it back to the parson*] A gift from Torkel to the poor. Go on—I'm giving it. It's just—because I don't go to church and yet I'm a Christian, you must understand.

TOLKENING: *lamely*] Yes . . . Well . . . . Alright . . . I'll announce it from the pulpit next Sunday.

TORKEL: No, no for Christ's sake! If you give your little mite, you should do it so that it's not seen by anybody. Right. I know that much!

TOLKENING: As you wish. This is—a very noble side to you.

TORKEL: Now I must be off. It's been a great pleasure for me! A really great pleasure. Reverend!

TOLKENING: Many thanks, Mr. Torkel. Hope you get home all right.

TORKEL: *out of the door*] I'll see to that. Well, then, good night, Mrs. Tolkening. [*off*].

ANITA *all this time has been standing by the great bay window as if turned to stone.*

TOLKENING *staggers up and down and finally collapses into a chair, burying his face in his hands.*

ANITA: *pulls herself together quickly, hurries over to him, strokes his hair with wide-spread fingers*] Don't be angry with me, Frederick. Please, don't be angry with me!

TOLKENING: *gets up weakly*] But this has got to come to an end. Yes, it must. It must come to an end.

ANITA: Yes—of course . . . Yes, of course it will. And—and—[*she blushes involuntarily*] tomorrow—or perhaps the day after tomorrow we'd better put your bed into my room. I've been meaning to say that to you.

TOLKENING: *smiles weakly; there are tears in his eyes*] You are such a good wife to me . . . There is something deep down inside you, striving towards our Great Lord. You see . . . maybe in the end you are not to blame for these things, maybe even there is no question of any guilt or blame involved. All I mean is— slaughtering all these little animals—after all they are such timorous creatures . . .

ANITA: *quickly*] Yes, yes. Of course. They are slaughtered—so very, very quickly, that they never feel anything.

TOLKENING: Because if I did not know that, Anita, I just wouldn't be able to stand it!

ANITA: You can rest assured. And — — now—at long last — — here comes our Dr. Joy and his little sister — — your—your childhood sweetheart — —

TOLKENING: *turns red*] Oh!

ANITA: It's going to be exciting—and—fun. Just wait. It'll all work out, you'll see.

A knock.

TOLKENING: *pulls himself together*] Come in! Come in!!

DR. JOY *steps in. You can tell from looking at him that he carries around his own completely formulated outlook on things. He is wearing sports clothes.*

TOLKENING: Well? Where's Agatha?

DR. JOY: She's still not quite ready. And as I didn't want to keep you waiting any longer— — —

ANITA: You were quite right to come on by yourself, doctor.

DR. JOY: Oh, come now: doctor, doctor. We mustn't be so formal—

ANITA: As you wish . . . I'll see if I can help your dear sister hurry along a little bit.

TOLKENING: Yes, that will be best, Anita!

DR. JOY: I'm sure that will give her the greatest pleasure, Mrs. Tolkening.

ANITA: *with excited pleasure*] And then we'll have some music and sing and dance and light the light-house. [*off*].

TOLKENING: Ha ha ha ha! Now we'll have a little glass of brandy. Come, John! It's the best you can get in the East.

DR. JOY: Light-house? Tell me, what's that all about?

TOLKENING: *filling the glasses*] Light-house? Oh yes—that's this bay window here. There's something very special about it. [*he puts down the decanter and steps forward to the bay window with* DR JOY] Somebody had the marvellous idea of building the parsonage and the church outside the village on this hill. You see from here the view is splendid. Down below you can see the great lake lying between the hills, and away at the back, quite small, but very clear, you can make out our nearest town. And if you have specially good eye-sight, you can just see the towers of the state capital far away against the horizon. But down below us here our garden takes you right down to the shores of the lake. There's the boat-house, buried in snow. And we light this lamp in the window in the evening and leave it burning till the morning. You see it serves as a light-house to all the local inhabitants of the district when they are crossing the lake or out fishing. It's a good and economical spirit lamp, you must know. And if the weather is particularly stormy, we hook up this highly polished mirror behind it. O—it really shines then, and sends its beams out through the night as if it were trying to out-shine the stars themselves, it's so bright it's a pure joy! And it's such a strange feeling to be sitting here, knowing that people are moving around the town and looking up and seeing our light-house.

DR. JOY. It certainly is a peculiar and really beautiful district.

TOLKENING: Yes. And here—right behind the village—that's where the great forests start, which, studded with swamps, reach far into the heart of Russia. The map gives no idea of it. You can keep on walking from here right to the Black Sea and probably even as far as Siberia without ever having to leave the forest. If you stand here quietly, you can feel the great heart of Asia pulsing in your veins.

DR. JOY: I'm sure the very thought of it must give you rather an uplifting feeling. Powerful personalities—like your wife for example—I can imagine—must tremble at the thought of being able at any given moment, to run out unfettered, deeper and deeper into the snow-covered ice-cracking wilderness!

TOLKENING: There is a good deal in what you are saying. Anita was born in one of the nearby villages. When she was a child these villages stood really deep in the forest.

DR. JOY: It was this—power that you found compelling?

TOLKENING: *smiles*] Yes—it really did compel me. And it is so glorious to let oneself be compelled by unfettered power.

DR. JOY: *hesitates*] Hm—yes. There does seem to be a very special kind of pleasure about it.

TOLKENING: There certainly is.

DR. JOY: *steps back to the table*] And you have no children . . .

TOLKENING: Nnno . . . We did have a little girl after a year. But she died very young . . . [*hesitates*] Anita has not much time for children, I think. And in the end maybe the child simply died because it wasn't loved enough—by its mother . . .

DR. JOY: That's true. They just dry up then . . .

TOLKENING: *slightly astonished*] Of course! That's just what happened

— — —

They sit facing each other. TOLKENING *raises his glass. They drink in silence.*

TOLKENING: I think you once wrote that you have no intention of ever getting married . . .

DR. JOY: Scarcely one marriage in a hundred is a happy one in Europe. And if you have been as severely punished by nature as

I have been then there is no prospect of a peaceful family life.

TOLKENING: Punished? I must say I've never noticed . . .

DR. JOY: You were always rather an innocent. Alas. My punishment is that I must gaze into the innermost heart of all things. Sometimes I feel as if I have an extra sense. That's probably what it is. Every Tom, Dick and Harry reveals to me in a fraction of a second the overwhelming sum of his deepest secrets . . . That's what makes life so difficult—and to keep silent . . . [*he leaps up in exasperation*] What concern of mine are all the mountains of secrets of people I don't even know!

TOLKENING: This is a serious argument against marriage. I can certainly appreciate that.

DR. JOY: Can you, though? Oh no! This is not the real reason. It lies much, much deeper. I don't mind talking about it. For the unfamiliarity which has grown up between us in these last ten years must be broken right from the start, Frederick Tolkening.

TOLKENING: Doubtless this is as it should be. [*he is breathlessly tensed*].

DR. JOY: Please don't misunderstand what I am going to say to you now. [*he is now seated*] In the normal marriage the wife must fear the man!

TOLKENING: *weakly*] Yes—yes. Naturally . . .

DR. JOY: That is a law nobody can go against. The man must seek the one woman for marriage, who is afraid of him! Because the wife, you must understand, wants to know *fear* in love.

TOLKENING: And what if this is not the case?

DR. JOY: Then the wife will despise the husband!

TOLKENING: *uneasily*] But—she must worship his mind!

DR. JOY: Woman worships the God of love. That is the Female Principle. Woman wants to be afraid, terror-stricken, when she is in love. For her the man must be so awesome, that she will want to die of terror on the spot!

TOLKENING: But—but I'm sure such men don't exist any more—I should think.

DR. JOY: Among us civilized Europeans there are certainly no such men. But there are Negroes and Chinese and other such repulsive men, like the one I saw outside earlier going across the yard.

TOLKENING: *with expressed shock*] Torkel—!

DR. JOY: Men like that can do anything, anything! Even those things denied to the beloved husband.

TOLKENING *stands up and takes a few unsteady steps.*

DR. JOY: Look. It's always this way with all creatures. The male is the feared. Eyes must glow, when he calls!

TOLKENING: But it's not like that anywhere, anywhere in Europe any more.

DR. JOY: Certainly not in the married state. And that's why the woman remains unsatisfied. [*stands up too*] And if she cannot find such power, then she tries to make up for it with numbers. And that we narrow-minded men then call promiscuity.

TOLKENING: But look here, there are women— — —

DR. JOY: Yes—who content themselves. In that case they do what the spiders do. They devour their males after the act, body and soul, do you understand?

TOLKENING: *walks up and down the room excitedly*] What you say is terrible.

DR. JOY: We have moved towards the life of the spirit in every respect. And woman has never followed us. Woman has stopped where she has always been since the beginning of time. And now we men no longer give satisfaction. And for the very reason that we still want to give satisfaction, we must subject the body to too much strain. But that is degeneration. For a man's testicles are a rupture! Nothing more. In the bright past of the early ages of man this rupture never existed. And—the rupture is growing bigger. There's no foreseeing what the end will be. [*the landscape in the background slowly sinks in the dusk*].

TOLKENING: *relieved*] I think your sister—and Anita—are coming.

DR. JOY: *urgently*] And the farther away we men get from the Prime Cause, the less woman is satisfied by us.

TOLKENING: !

DR. JOY: And another thing, do you know who is to blame for this whole dreadful state of affairs?

TOLKENING *his astonishment growing.*

DR. JOY: You! YOU!! You!!!—Or—if you prefer—Him, in whose name you go among men! Him! Christ!! I wager it has never occurred to you that all the great religions of the world are conceived always for men alone. For woman always remains untouched by the great messages of salvation. And Moses . . .

AGATHA JOY *and* ANITA *come in.*

TOLKENING: *desperately tries to make a joke*] How splendid, you've arrived just at the right moment. John Joy was just in the process of crushing me absolutely under a mountain of words.

AGATHA: *a sweet little blonde, gives him her hand*] What a marvellous place you live in. And that must be the light-house you were telling me about, Mrs. Tolkening.

TOLKENING: Yes, that's it.

ANITA: I find all this luke-warm Christianity really disgraceful. What's the point of it all, if some people see nothing wrong in our giving some of our best friends the not so attractive side of the house. Though it is still very pleasant, of course.

TOLKENING *speechless.*

DR. JOY: *slowly, with emphasis*] Modern weaklings like us can't do anything about it, Mrs. Tolkening.

ANITA: I'm sure you are right. Don't you think so, Tolkening?

TOLKENING: I don't know what you mean ... Let's have some supper.

AGATHA: I'm still so tired, that I really couldn't take anything, except perhaps a glass of tea, if you don't mind. [*they begin to take their places round the table while* TOLKENING *fills the tea-glasses*].

TOLKENING: You see, our housekeeper is spending the night in the village.

ANITA: Yes—her daughter had a baby last night.

AGATHA: *looking out the window*] It really is lovely up here on the hilltop.

ANITA: And tomorrow we'll both drive out into the forests with the troika. With no bells! For you mustn't scare away the creatures and weird figures in all that thick growth.

AGATHA *and* ANITA *exchange glances.* AGATHA'S *is surprised.*

DR. JOY: I've only just realized you even have a gun there.

TOLKENING: Yes—and it is a very good rifle, needless to say. But— naturally—I don't shoot. I've scratched 'Misericordia' on the barrel.

ANITA: How could you imagine that a parson like him would squeeze the butt of a gun against his cheek! And you certainly wouldn't hit anything. But in the depths of the forests there are terrible hunters with great big black beards, out and out bandits nobody ever catches sight of. When I was a girl there was one they called Red Breast, because he had red hair on his chest, just imagine. Red hair! How ghastly that must have been.

TOLKENING: You shouldn't talk about these bandits, they don't exist outside the heads of young girls. Miss Joy has gone quite pale.

ANITA: Once they raided our village, when I was in the city. They dragged off all the women. And next day the women all came back quite hale and hearty. [*animatedly*] Just imagine: the bandits hadn't touched them. Gave them gifts of gold and silver and let them go. They were real men in those days!! Yes . . .

AGATHA: *trembling, pale, her eyes burning*] Do you really have that kind of thing here?

TOLKENING: Once upon a time probably—same as anywhere else— and here it lasted a little longer than in other parts of the country. And because life is so slow here, it all lives on bright and fresh in local memory. Usually I like to hear of these things. Because there is still something of the overgrown child about me, liking to feel his nearness to the terrifying old tales and sagas.

ANITA: *bursts out laughing and gives a quick cough to cover up her laughter*] You are a great dreamer, Tolkening. Just think, he even has great dreams in the day-time.

TOLKENING: Yes, sometime I lie down specially, just to dream for a moment. And I've just written a large book about the dream-life of human beings.

DR. JOY: *who has sat down*] I can well believe it. Here in East Prussia there is just so much TIME.

TOLKENING: Actually I have a great deal to do.

DR. JOY: To do. Of course! That's something quite different. I mean: here there is in the true sense of the word an extraordinary amount of TIME! And you must let me read your manuscript.

TOLKENING: Gladly, gladly. I've come across some quite peculiar things, which will also be of interest to the medical man.

ANITA: You really can't be pressed, Miss Joy?

AGATHA *declines.*

ANITA: Then—maybe the two of us—should— — —

A long drawn out raucous howl echoes gruesomely from outside.

ANITA: That's just what I meant! [*she stands up*].

TOLKENING *gives* ANITA *a frightened look.*

AGATHA *who has sprung out of her seat now stares speechless at* TOLKENING *with a look of horror.*

DR. JOY *has dropped his knife and fork with a clatter and stopped chewing.*

TOLKENING: *slowly*] Please, don't be so frightened. Everything is quite in order. We just haven't mentioned yet that we have wolves— — —

AGATHA: *in great terror*] There are wolves here?

DR. JOY: Real wolves? In broad daylight? [*he stands up*] This is something I must see.

TOLKENING: *holds him back*] No, no. You'll never get a glimpse of them out in the open. They only very rarely come out of the great depths of the forests, and even then they only appear singly in very hard winters, although they have been coming in unusual numbers last year and even more in this.

AGATHA: Well, then—where are the wolves that just howled?

ANITA: Just come along with me, Agatha. I'll show you the wolves. Don't be afraid. You can see them through the bars. There is absolutely no danger.

TOLKENING: Yes—absolutely none. And I'll show them to you too afterwards, John.

DR. JOY: This is certainly quite astonishing. Yes—of course! Go along, my dear child. Standing face to face with the beasts is the best way to get over your fear of them.

TOLKENING: And besides we decided earlier this evening that the beasts have to be got rid of.

ANITA: Got rid of?—Yes—maybe we shall get rid of them. One of them at least. Yes— — maybe you could—shoot one of them.

TOLKENING: Me?—Well—maybe somebody else will.

ANITA: Somebody else? Oh—just think how he might torture the poor beast!

TOLKENING: That's a question that will bear some examination. You can't expect me to murder a caged animal that can't escape and can't defend itself.

ANITA: Then they will just have to keep on living.

AGATHA: *throws a quick, penetrating look at her brother. She stands up and goes*] Come along then, if you want to . . .

ANITA: *following her excitedly*] It is fearfully exciting, I can tell you. *Both off.*

DR. JOY *has stopped eating and is walking slowly up and down the room.*

TOLKENING *sitting and looking silently at the floor.*

During the course of this exchange night begins to fall.

DR. JOY *stops*] How many are there in your menagerie?

TOLKENING: Two wolves; a he and a she. It's really quite harmless. Strangely enough, however, they have been the cause of more and more minor differences between Anita and me lately.

DR. JOY: And how in all the world did you ever capture these beasts?!

TOLKENING: They are certainly fearfully difficult to capture. Anita got them as a present about two years ago—from the unpleasant character you saw outside earlier. They were quite small then— like little dogs. There are lonely foresters out in the woods, who keep young wolves as watch dogs. Of course—when they get too big, they have to be killed.

DR. JOY: This is really fascinating! And so you have brought up these two wolves . . .

TOLKENING: Yes—we have. Or rather Anita has looked after everything herself. She has a weakness for odd things. And if it's something in any way dangerous—even if it's only the tiniest little bit dangerous—that's exactly what she likes best.

DR. JOY: And that means these beasts must have eaten their way through whole mountains of meat in the last couple of years.

TOLKENING: No, I don't think so. If you were to put everything over the whole period onto one pile—yes—well, it probably would look a lot. But the peasants of the district brought dead cats, crows and other refuse they had no use for. They were always very willing and ready to help us keep both wolves fed. The people sort of liked the idea that the parsonage had wolves as house pets.

DR. JOY: And now they have grown big and strong.

TOLKENING: Yes—they certainly have. And especially the he-wolf. He is a splendid animal. The she-wolf looks a bit starved, because she never seems to want to eat.

DR. JOY: I see . . . I see . . . And what's to become of the animals now? [*he has sat down again*].

TOLKENING: *looks at him in surprise. After a short silence, with hesitation*] I must admit—there are considerable difficulties we had not even thought of at the start.

DR. JOY: Difficulties—?

TOLKENING: Yes—you see the village people seem to have suddenly turned against the animals, do you understand . . .

DR. JOY: One could appreciate that they . . .

TOLKENING: Yes, yes. But then they should give us time to get rid of the creatures.

DR. JOY: *lost in thought*] Who knows how this all hangs together . . .

TOLKENING: *with a start*] Eh!—I mean, suddenly they don't bring any more food for the animals, because they say they could be a danger to the district. And I tell you—they are quite securely locked up. And Anita really has them so much in the palm of her hand that they are as obedient—as trusty hounds. Especially the he-wolf. The she-wolf is inclined to snap, it's true.

DR. JOY: So if I understand you right—you have placed yourself into rather peculiar opposition to your congregation . . . That is certainly very awkward.

TOLKENING: Yes—it certainly is. But the people must show some sense! I can't just let the beasts loose. Just imagine what a catastrophe that would be!

DR. JOY: Why don't you just have them killed!?

TOLKENING: *gets up and begins to pace up and down*] You know—I keep ducks and hens and lambs. I love these creatures with all my being. They eat out of my hand, and it is a pure joy, when I go across the yard. And—when I'm wearing my robes on Sunday and step out from the house here to the church, the whole pack of little scamps comes cackling and gabbling, hopping and dancing after me; the lambs rub up against my legs—I don't want to exaggerate. You'll see for yourself what joy there is in the congregation when they see it. I think I can say without boasting that I am the most popular parson in the diocese and that people even drive over from remote parishes and our church is often too small to hold all the congregation.

DR. JOY: I believe you— — —

TOLKENING: But can you believe that I'd have one of these creatures killed for food? No, John, I would not. They are to live till they die naturally, or if that is painful, I give them to some poor person. I love them too much.

DR. JOY: And your wife shares this love of animals?

TOLKENING: *sits down again*] Well, look, it's like this. She loves the untamed so much—or—how shall I put it. She does not particularly share my love of defenceless creatures. The wolves now, the wolves—she loves them passionately. And because it would hurt

126

her so fearfully we have not got rid of them. I don't want to—lay down the law about this. Because it could easily lead to lasting ill-feeling afterwards.

DR. JOY: But you'll have to do it sooner or later.

TOLKENING: Yes—there's a sort of strange silent warfare being waged with the villagers. Because they will certainly never tell me straight out what they want. They like me far too much for that. And that's why—at least it seems so to me—the whole battle is waged in the mind. It always looks in fact as if the really crucial point of the whole story is not visible to the eye. I'm sure you won't understand this.

DR. JOY: I understand it only too well, I can tell you!

TOLKENING: *surprised*] I see!—And what would you advise me to do, then?

DR. JOY: Before I answer that I'll have to ask a few questions.

TOLKENING: Everything is exactly as I told you . . .

DR. JOY: I'm sure it is. And you sum it up perfectly when you say you have the impression there's more going on in the mind than the eye can see. This seems to me very probable. All men have an extraordinary sensitivity for the psychic stirrings of their fellow-men. They are unconsciously guided by the monstrous principle that one betrays by silence one's most secret thoughts to the whole world.

TOLKENING: This is doubtless true. But I don't understand what this should have to do with the wolves.

DR. JOY: *brooding*] The wolves . . . The wolves . . .

TOLKENING *gets up and paces slowly this way and that as if in fearful expectation.*

DR. JOY: Tell me, Tolkening, who feeds the beasts?

TOLKENING: Anita has always done that herself. And you can take it from me she is always very keen about it. And I feed the lambs—naturally, as she can't do everything after all and the old housekeeper wouldn't get through it all on her own.

DR. JOY: *brooding*] And she throws the dead game into the cage for them . . .

TOLKENING: That's it—exactly. And I have impressed on everybody that not a single creature may suffer in any way because of these wolves. The creatures—and generally they are harmful creatures—are slaughtered so very, very quickly that they never notice.

DR. JOY: It's very comforting for you to know that. I can well imagine.

TOLKENING: Yes—because otherwise it would be unbearable.

DR. JOY: And the she-wolf—you say—is not thriving at all?

TOLKENING: Nnno . . . You know—what, er, conclusion I've come to?

DR. JOY: ?

TOLKENING: That Anita does not like the she-wolf so much. And I can understand why completely. Because the he-wolf, you see, is an extraordinarily powerful and beautiful beast. He has a really splendid coat and a truly terrifying mouth.

DR. JOY: And there haven't been any cubs bred?

TOLKENING: *in astonishment*] Eh—what are you thinking of. How could there be! Maybe there is a slightly [*smiling*] spicy flavour about the whole business. Because Anita is terribly anxious and careful never to let the two beasts come together.

DR. JOY: You mean—they are caged separately?

TOLKENING: Of course—the blacksmith made us a grille. And so they can't get to each other.

DR. JOY: I see—I see—[*short silence*] I must say this is an absorbing story.

TOLKENING: Yes—it certainly is. And you'll see for yourself how Anita glows when she comes back.

DR. JOY: Does she?

TOLKENING: Well—you can imagine, as this naturally excites her. Because going into the cage is not without a bit of danger. You see—and it's this unusual strength and power about Anita that enslaved me, as I said to you earlier.

DR. JOY: *gets up as well*] Tell me, Tolkening, will you—and please excuse this intimate question: what would you rather give up, if you were forced to choose: your wife—or Christ?

TOLKENING: *petrified*] That's—that's—a monstrous question, Joy! Holy Scripture— — —

DR. JOY:—says this and that, I know that already. But it also says a lot of other stuff the clergy have not grasped yet and probably, being clergy, never will.

TOLKENING: I've made up my mind not to argue with you about that. But by way of an answer I'll say this: I'll give up neither Christ nor my wife.

DR. JOY: Can't you see, Fredcrick Tolkening, that she is devouring you body and soul? She needs a bandit, do you understand me, a bandit with red hair on his chest!

TOLKENING: *smiles slightly*] You mean, I suppose, I should have taken Agatha.

DR. JOY: O—my little sister! The weak ones need the bandit with the hairy red chest even more!

TOLKENING: Mm yes—then in that case I don't know what you want, as I am still a married man.

DR. JOY: I'll tell you what you should do, Tolkening. [*quietly and urgently*] Now—right now—when she comes in, you should go out and strike the strong, splendid he-wolf dead with an axe!

TOLKENING: I should kill this beast which has done absolutely no wrong, just like that?

DR. JOY: Yes—Tolkening, you should! Completely brutal and heartless, split its skull! You should smash and crush the beast to pulp!

TOLKENING: Please calm down, John. That I certainly will not do.

DR. JOY: Then do you know there is no help for you, my dear fellow? Don't you know that she has started to devour you from the legs up?

TOLKENING: *firmly*] You are excited. You find me different from what you thought. You have forgotten yourself. I shall certainly be careful never to touch upon this point again. And—I praise married life as the Apostle Paul commends it to us—

DR. JOY: Paul! Yes, yes! Old Paul! It's unbelievable the wrong he has done mankind, he suppressed or failed to understand what Christ said to you: And the enemies of man will be members of his own household—repeating the words of the prophet who cries out in the same verse: 'Shut the door of your mouth against her who sleeps in your arms!' O God! Why won't you understand all that! Why do you run away so blindly and without misgiving or shame from the consequences of your Christianity. For the church and the theatre have up till now been there only for men, although it's women who particularly frequent these institutions. Why?!—just because they must somehow find a way out of the maze of contradictions their eternally unchanging flesh constantly forces upon them.

TOLKENING: *totally crushed*] I—don't know—what I—should think of this, John Joy . . .

DR. JOY: Why do you keep the fact from the poor people, that women live unconsciously in the subconscious eternal desire to be raped some day by a gorilla? It's there in the universe, why don't you say so? Why, it's as if this Jesus must have known the whole German Siegfried legend by heart. There must be somebody somewhere, who will speak out what men have suppressed or what they cannot or may not say!! If this is said openly, Tolkening, then things are not quite so bad . . . Because when something is expressed openly, then somehow it slowly begins to regulate itself . . .

AGATHA: *comes into the room very quickly. She stops and suppresses her extreme agitation*] O—that was—horrible—I could not stand it!

DR. JOY: And so you ran away . . .

AGATHA: Yes—otherwise I should have—probably fainted . . .

TOLKENING: There's no doubt it's not something for weak nerves.

DR. JOY: Agatha's nerves are not a bit weak.

AGATHA: I've seen wilder and more ferocious beasts—and even— touched them. [*with a shudder*] But it was a different, strange, quite distinct feeling of horror that came over me. [*with staring eyes*] The air seemed heavy with some curious kind of battle.

TOLKENING: Battle?

AGATHA: *gives him a quick look*] I don't know.

TOLKENING: Were they fed?

AGATHA: Yes—the she-wolf—a piece of meat. And she devoured it at one gulp. And the he-wolf was terribly angry, because he did not get anything. He—must—have a clean snout—Mrs. Tolkening said . . .

TOLKENING: Yes—Anita is very particular with the beasts, exactly like me with my lambs.

AGATHA *stares him in the face in amazement.*

DR. JOY: A—piece—of meat—

AGATHA: O—there were some rabbits too—

DR. JOY: Rabbits?

TOLKENING: Yes—since the locals stopped giving us food for the animals we've—now and again—filled in with a rabbit.

AGATHA: *her astonishment increasing*] But—throwing the poor creatures to the beasts like that . . . I certainly would not put up with that. And it didn't happen today.

TOLKENING: Well—they are already slaughtered after all . . .

DR. JOY *has fixed* AGATHA *with his gaze.*

AGATHA: *surprised*] Yes—yes. Somebody slaughters them.

DR. JOY *sinks into his chair in torment.*

TOLKENING: And now it's time we forgot about those wolves . . . [*he steps over to the bay-window*] Just a few minutes of this sun-set, then we'll light the light-house. Lots of people have gone sleighing across the lake.

ANITA: *comes in, drying her hands with a handkerchief*] What did you run away for, Miss Joy? I had a few things still to tell you.

DR. JOY: *lost in thought*] All these charming and so sensitive little rabbits.

AGATHA: *started*] Nobody said anything!

ANITA: *turns away with biting contempt*] Ha ha! You weaklings . . .

TOLKENING: *turns back from the window to the room, lost in thought and says*] I—don't—understand— —

ANITA: *speaking more and more slowly and as if possessed, as the action continues*] There is a man in the village—not Torkel, he would never ever do this kind of thing—this man never misses a Sunday in the church, and kneels and prays before and after meals and sings hymns night and morning, so that they really ring out! He is a truly devout and faithful Christian, as everybody knows! And I have actually seen him torturing cats till they died and killing rabbits and skinning them before the very eyes of the other rabbits waiting their turn.

TOLKENING: *eyes staring in amazement*] Is—that—really true?

ANITA: *viciously*] What's the point of your Christianity, if there are things like that—or if it does not take account of the beast that slumbers hidden in the human breast! [*the long drawn out howl of a wolf close by the window. All, with the exception of* ANITA, *are for a moment rigid with terror*].

TOLKENING: Great God—something must have gone wrong. [*he steps quickly into the deep window area*] The—she-wolf is loose! The she-wolf is loose! You must have forgotten to lock the gate!!

ANITA: *for something to say*] You must be imagining things, Tolkening.

TOLKENING: *rebelling slightly*] You don't like the she-wolf, Anita.

ANITA: You must be making a mistake, Tolkening.

TOLKENING: Dear God! Now she's running down to the lake!

DR. JOY: *has leapt to his feet*] Would you ever dream it was possible . . .

AGATHA: There could easily be a dreadful accident!

ANITA: That's not at all unlikely; if there are children sleighing on the lake . . . I think you will have to shoot her.

TOLKENING: Yes—of course—I must shoot her! Shoot her immediately! And if I miss, we must alert the villagers.

ANITA: *feigning sympathy*] O God! those people will stab it to death with pitchforks.

TOLKENING: I'll aim well if it is not too dark already. I'll just get my cap. [*about to go off*].

DR. JOY: I have a good revolver, Tolkening. Naturally I won't let you go alone.

TOLKENING: Good. [*off*].

AGATHA: *in growing alarm*] If it's always like this here . . .

ANITA: *making a slight attempt to calm her*] No—no—it's not always like this here. Each day different from the one before. I think it's the same everywhere.

DR. JOY: Yes. Yes. It's the same everywhere. What we want is not allowed and what we don't want seems to possess us.

ANITA *and* AGATHA *give him a chilling look*.

TOLKENING: *in fur coat and cap*] Now we can get a move on.

DR. JOY: Yes—we'd better.

ANITA: Won't you get very warm in that coat?

TOLKENING: *has taken the gun down carefully*] No!—I have cartridges in my pocket.

DR. JOY: *as he goes out*] Then you can wait for me at the door.

TOLKENING: *follows him*] You get your revolver.

ANITA: Shoot to kill, Tolkening! Just imagine the terrible torment of the poor beast hurt out there in bitter frost with a gaping wound!

TOLKENING: I shall do my best, you can believe me. [*he goes out handling the gun gingerly*].

ANITA: *stretches her limbs with a smile*] The she-wolf . . . The she-wolf . . .

AGATHA: *choking*] I'm— — afraid of you, Mrs. Tolkening, throwing live rabbits to the wolves.

ANITA: You see how wrong one can be. These smart blood-hounds like your brother, for example, are terribly easy to deceive. [*seriously*] For I never have done what is in your mind, Miss Joy!

AGATHA: *surprised*] No?

ANITA: And even if I am—a little bandit—or a bandit's bride—as you wish—you should remember bandits are basically the *best* people.

AGATHA: I really don't know anything about that, Mrs. Tolkening.

ANITA: Women should not be so secretive with each other . . . Do you play the piano?

AGATHA: *disconcerted*] No . . . But—I have a bass and I love to strike a few chords on it from time to time.

ANITA: *intent, comes closer*] A bass! Yes—the bass is good. And we could play a regular Murki together occasionally.

AGATHA *uneasy, goes to the table.*

ANITA: But now we shall light the light-house.—Look, the sun has set long since, and the clouds are still standing like red shrines as far as the middle of the sky. [*she has pushed a chair into position and lights the lamp in the window*] And then we'd better hook on the mirror right away; and we can chat in the twilight—till the—men come back. [*a great roaring laugh of triumph, echoing up from far out over the lake, can be heard quite clearly*].

ANITA: *steps back into the room startled*] That—was—Torkel . . .

AGATHA: What was? What *was* that? Has she attacked somebody?

ANITA: She is indescribably starved; so it is difficult to tell exactly.

AGATHA: But that was a roar of laughter, unless I'm mistaken . . .

ANITA: People round here laugh all the time at the most curious things . . .

AGATHA: *withdraws to the bench by the stove*] No—you know—it's really uncanny in this house . . .

ANITA: *comes up to the table too and sits down*] Oh—you mustn't say that. A woman has to adapt herself to the general framework. And the narrower the frame the more exciting she must make it for herself. Isn't it marvellous that human beings have heads with which they can work all this out so precisely?

AGATHA: I noticed on the way here that women up here are basically violent by nature, even if they don't show it so very much.

ANITA: Women up here are doubtless the same as anywhere else, it's just that in the western cities— — they think more like Christians— — Tell me, is it possible to love a Christian?

AGATHA: What on earth do you mean?

ANITA: I don't mean *Christian* exactly. I mean, are there in the cities and out in the country too for that matter still men—for us . . . I

133

mean—men—the kind of men, you just need to see and you're on fire, ablaze!—Because that's what really counts . . .

AGATHA: I've never seen a man like that.

ANITA: Because a Christian—you know—I call all civilized men Christians—a mere Christian you can just make a fool of. And in the end you fall into it because there is no other way.

AGATHA: But I'm a good Christian myself, you can believe me.

ANITA: Go on! You little Christian, you! All that means is making oneself smaller than one really is, so that it's easier to feel terrified by the male.

AGATHA: O—surely it's enough—if we know—deep down—who the real boss is.

ANITA: So that's it! A gentle miss and a big bass, there must be some connection somewhere. And in the end you'll be doing men's work. And at the very finish you'll live my life, mine, mine, mine!— — And your words will stare at you like corpses . . .

AGATHA: *tries nervously to get up*] You do so delight in saying these things . . .

ANITA: What are you afraid of anyway? What is there for a woman to be afraid of, tell me! What we fear is exactly what we seek. It is the indescribably dark deep down in our hated flesh. We *want* to be raped. That's the answer. We *want* to be raped! But we try to flee. It is so wonderful to flee knowing we'll be caught. In the end we want to be caught and ripped open. [*her eyes are staring wide and there is a rattle in her throat*].

AGATHA: You do so delight in saying these things!

ANITA: To be raped to death. How wonderful—

The wolf howls from its cage.

ANITA: *stands up and stretches her full height*] The wolf . . . the wolf . . . He is howling for the mate he never got! [*a shudder runs through her whole body*].

AGATHA: *sinks trembling and half-unconscious against the stove.*

ANITA: *notices, as she slowly turns*] O! You are unwell. [*smiling*] What an unusual climax . . .

AGATHA: I have a headache. And—I'm—so tired . . .

ANITA: *briskly*] You should have a sleep—you really should. Here on this bench. It is very wide. I'll bring you a few covers. I won't disturb you at all . . . I've got various things to do . . .

You really could have a sleep—till the—men come back.

AGATHA: Perhaps I could stretch out a little . . .

ANITA: Of course! You should. New experiences are so tiring. [*she goes into her room, leaves the door open, lights a lamp in there and comes back with covers*].

ANITA: You're really not supposed to wrap yourself up in other people's blankets. You never know the regular dreams and thoughts of the person they belong to. I suffered from nightmares for ages because I had to sleep in the blankets of somebody evil. It's true . . .

AGATHA: *weakly*] I don't believe in that kind of thing, Mrs. Tolkening. You must never forget my brother is a doctor.

ANITA: O! Doctors . . .

The tremendous muffled thud of an explosion in the distance.

AGATHA sits up with a start and stares at ANITA in terror.

ANITA: There you go getting scared again, because you don't know what it is . . . That's the frost, Miss Joy. It's freezing so hard that the ice in the lake is bursting. It leaves long, wide cracks through several feet of ice. It will keep you awake all night. To me it sounds like a lullaby.

AGATHA: *forlornly*] What terrible country, Mrs. Tolkening.

ANITA: *she is already speaking maddeningly slowly*] You have no idea how pleased I am to hear you say that. And then there are great elks in the moors of this country. Beasts with great antlers, bigger than horses and so dangerous when they're in rut.

AGATHA: They thrust with these terrible horns . . .

ANITA: No—they don't. They kick with their front hooves and they are so powerful with two, three kicks they smash horses or carts to smithereens!

AGATHA: *admiringly*] And Mr. Tolkening dares to go out there into the dangers of the night.

ANITA: Oh! Come on, now! Don't try to make yourself smaller than you really are. And before Tolkening of all people, ha ha! [*she has stepped over to the piano and idly plays a few notes*] You know—there are songs here, which hang on such an unresolved, plaintive note, they stop as if they still weren't finished.

AGATHA: That's—quite awful. I've heard them. They unsettle your whole being and after the song you feel so fearfully lonely.

ANITA: That's exactly how it is. It's wonderful the way your whole being is unsettled. [*she strikes this kind of note several times and lets it fade away*] It's so lovely it makes you want to howl. I always feel as if all the unquenched desires of the Eternal Eve are compressed into this one note . . . Wouldn't you like to hear one of those songs?

AGATHA: For heaven's sake—no. That's a little too much all at once.

ANITA: O—that's how it is here every day; really nothing—and yet so very much.—But now you should try to sleep . . . Look, I'm closing the partition. Now it is quite dark in the room. And I can scarcely see where you lie. Wait. Just one more little crack. Now you can scarcely see a shadow. Just look around. Can you see me? [*she has closed the door-curtain to the light-house. It is now scarcely possible to make her out*].

AGATHA: *who has made herself comfortable on the broad bench in the meantime, with tired voice*] No. I see nothing. So suddenly dark. I'm so—terribly—tired— —

The ice rumbles.

ANITA: *very comforting and slow*] Do you hear? That's the ice rumbling. In time you'll find it beautiful. Don't be afraid of it. It is all, all, quite, quite safe . . . [*she falls silent and goes slowly to her room. A very dim beam of light appears, as she opens the door. She notices the light the lamp sheds and goes purposefully into her room, closing the door behind her*].

For a considerable while everything is still. Suddenly AGATHA *utters a horrible scream.*

Silence.

ANITA: *opens the door again. The beam of light is no longer there. She glides in quietly in nightdress, a scarcely visible shadow. Whispering*] What are you screaming for, Miss Joy?

No answer.

ANITA: She's asleep . . . dreaming . . . [*she leaves the door open and crosses quickly over to the other side and leaves the room through the door to the yard*].

For a considerable while everything is still. The disturbed breathing of the sleeping woman can be heard. The ice rumbles. The heavy breathing stops. The house door creaks slightly.

ANITA *comes back in. Only her shadow can be seen and beside it the shadow of a great, strong beast she is leading beside her. The rattle of a heavy chain can be heard briefly once. Once in her room, she closes*

136

the door quickly.

AGATHA: *shoots upright with a jolt. In a choking, rapid whisper*] The—the—wolf! But that's impossible. [*she has leapt up, gropes to the curtain and opens it a little. She is shivering as if in a high fever. Her eyes are great staring orbs. Her face is distorted with nameless terror*] That is—monstrous! Oh God! Oh God! What am I to do! [*she drags herself with all the signs of crazed terror to the way out*] This is unbearable. This is absolutely unbearable!

Sounds of disturbance can be heard from the next room.

AGATHA: *sinks backwards against the wall and in blind desperation keeps beating her head against it*] God Almighty!— — God Almighty!— Scream! Scream! [*still suppressed*] The wolf! What is she doing with the wolf!

Just as she is pulling herself up, to rush out of the door, through the same door. TORKEL *slips in as quietly and quickly as an eel. He stands there huge and broad and stares at the girl in amazement. His clothing has been ripped from the throat, his chest is completely bare. He has no cap.*

AGATHA: *retreats a few weak steps in horror and stares at the man open-mouthed*] He—he—help—can't you!

TORKEL: *himself a little confused, also speaks quietly*] Wh-what? Just don't be afraid, my timid little bird. I'm Torkel, in case you should ever have heard of me. That's just a little blood on my hands. But it's wolf's blood, right. Just don't be afraid. If Torkel is there, then you are *absolutely* SAFE, I can tell you. And my coat is really alright! The beast just ripped it a bit, that's all. You can bet it's paid for with its life. Pity. Pity . . . 'Cause the wolf is a noble creature, strong, rough like the weather and the woods it lives and flourishes in! Yes—

The noise has become more violent meanwhile.

TORKEL: With women, you know, I speak properly. But there's no need for the men to know what Torkel is capable of.—Is Mrs. Anita Tolkening not at home, strange lady?—

AGATHA: *has retreated as far as the bay window and stands there as if petrified. Suddenly in an explosion of terror she screams out*] Go in there! Quickly! Quickly! She has the wolf, the wolf in her room!

TORKEL: *dumbfounded*] The— —wolf?— [*a fit of choking comes over him. Rage pours over his face. He lowers his head like a bull, going into battle*].

A piercing scream from ANITA *in the next room breaks off abruptly.*

137

Violent noise. Shattering window.

AGATHA: Something has happened in there! [*she has come back to the bench and collapses on it unconscious*].

TORKEL: *goes up to* ANITA'S *room, quickly and heavily. He opens the door. Steps inside. Laughs violently. Stays there a moment. Comes back, his face taut. Dully*] On the bed naked! And with—her throat ripped open—her throat ripped open!— — Up there round her throat was so white and full for the teeth! [*remembers in silence*] I've seen that once before. Poor—Anita . . . [*he sobs*] Even Torkel wasn't strong enough . . . And this lovely girl didn't die of fright . . . [*he goes to the curtain, fumbles around and pulls it up*].

AGATHA: *moves, leaps up and screams at him*] Why don't you go in there?—The Wolf!

TORKEL: Everything is alright. Everything in its place, timid little bird . . . The Wolf? He's jumped through the window. That's all, you can believe . . .

AGATHA: *stares absently at his naked chest and suddenly shudders*] You have such red hair—on your chest.

TORKEL: That's all the many woods and all the many weathers. And the foresters don't believe what I say . . . [*compels her with his eye*] Take away—and then bring back. That's what Torkel can do. If you ever have a special wish, something difficult up here— there's always something—then you just need to give Torkel the wink. These pale white thin men are not worthwhile. [*he holds his arm with the rolled-up sleeve against the light and gives his body a jerk*] And he can make the hairs on his arm stand up straight, Torkel can—look . . .

AGATHA *stares at his arm with rapt horror.*

TORKEL: Life or Death—every day. And always as inscrutable as the grave . . . [*he cocks his ear*] Here come the—men . . . Yes—here they come . . . There's no need for them to know I'm here. So I'll go out—the way of the wolf. Farewell! And don't forget I know places in the woods no human has ever seen . . . Take away and bring back . . . That's what Torkel is good at . . . Nobody knows that—or ever will—dear little dove . . . [*he leaves through the door to* ANITA'S *room*].

The front door creaks. The voices of TOLKENING *and* DR. JOY *can be heard. A heavy object drops on the floor in the hall.*

TOLKENING *and* DR. JOY *come in.*

TOLKENING: I hope you have not been afraid, dear Miss . . .

AGATHA: Oh . . . I . . .

DR. JOY *is surprised and fixes her sharply with his eye.*

TOLKENING: Wasn't there a man in this room?

AGATHA: *frantic, stares out her brother]* Nnno . . .

She sinks into her seat.

DR. JOY: *deeply shaken]* Sister!

AGATHA: *stares around, her eyes flickering uncertainly]* Take away—
and then bring back . . . [*muffled*] That's what he's goo— —
[*piercing scream*] The wolf!

TOLKENING: What's all this? [*he strides as if intoxicated towards* ANITA'S
room].

AGATHA: *in sweet terror]* M— — Mother — —! The Wolves— — —
The Wolves— — — —

As TOLKENING *is just on the point of opening the door, the curtain falls.*

SQUIRE BLUE BOLL

by Ernst Barlach

1926

Translated by J. M. Ritchie

Characters:

LANDOWNER BOLL
HIS WIFE
GRETA GRÜNTAL
HER HUSBAND
OTTO PRUNKHORST
SHOEMAKER HOLTFRETER
WATCHMAKER VIRGIN
MAYOR
ELIAS
HIS WIFE DORIS
A GENTLEMAN
MRS UNK
GUESTS
COACHMAN SAUGWURM
PEOPLE
THREE DEAD MEN
WEHDIG
PIPELOW

I

Market-place with shops, in the background the base of the church tower with great portal arch. Boll and wife cross the market-place.

BOLL: *stops*] Still light mist—really not at all unpleasant—eh, Martha?

MRS. BOLL: Except for the shivers—etcetera—when we were driving down Krönkhagen, I began to feel perhaps it was maybe just a teeny-weeny bit too nippy.

BOLL: Quite right, Martha—still, look at that hazy perspective—I quite like it—there might be more behind it than you think—things might not go according to plan—and anyway, what's the point in the long run of a smooth life with a guarantee of no legs broken—what do you say, Martha?

MRS. BOLL: I don't know and nobody can know what the good of it might be if things turn out different from the way you think, but that's still no reason at all for me to aim at that, and forget the respect I owe myself—I understand our dear Lord far too well to think that His intentions for me might be quite different from what I can appreciate—no—oh, no!

BOLL: Well, this is the shop—Bierhals & Co.! Shall I risk being snubbed by the salesgirl. She provides the good taste, you make the decision, and I—what do you need me for?

MRS. BOLL: Now, Kurt, you know very well we must dig up something suitable for Auntie Emma's birthday.

BOLL: Quite right, Martha, this is one of those cases which may be a matter of life and death—so, what with my tendency to high blood pressure and dizzy spells—you see, Martha, you do see that, I see—don't you, Martha? But may I open the door for you? [opens the door].

MRS. BOLL: What else was there, Kurt . . . yes, and then we have arranged to dine with the Prunkhorsts, and Otto and Bertha are always so charmingly punctual for that kind of thing and that obliges us to be the same—don't go on like that, Kurt. [she disappears].

BOLL: hesitates to himself] The air is heavy with it, the air brings it and the air delivers it up. [follows her].

HOLTFRETER and GRÜNTAL meet.

GRÜNTAL: What a surprise, Uncle Holtfreter!

HOLTFRETER: Lo and behold, it's Grüntal, just imagine: Grüntal!

GRÜNTAL: And now—what now?

HOLTFRETER: Yes, what can one do about it, Grüntal; leave well alone. If Greta has run away from home, Greta will come back again for sure, leave well alone. Yes, she has been to my place, came and wept and wept and wept . . .

GRÜNTAL: Then everything is alright—you can come right back with me, Uncle Holtfreter, and I can fetch her from your place—have to get back to Parum, you can just imagine how the children are howling!

HOLTFRETER: You'll have to find Greta for yourself—when I left she didn't look as if she was going to stay there weeping. 'Uncle,' she says, 'you go out, Uncle, I want to go out too,' she says—what has gone wrong with her this time, is she getting her ideas again? Ideas, Grüntal, are things you don't know about—you know? Is she on about flesh again this time too?

GRÜNTAL: You can rely on it—flesh is her only trouble. Away with flesh, she often says to the children—bacon and ham and sausages, she says, will turn *you* into bacon and sausages. Are you a lot of bellies, or what? And she puts her hands over her ears like this and asks: 'Can't you hear what they are saying,' and she means the children, and if I ask she says, 'Be quiet and let them moan, let them scream—they shall have their will.' That's what it's like at our place, you see.

HOLTFRETER: Yes, I see.

GRÜNTAL: 'Why,' she says, 'getting fat is what fat stock are there for, so it is part of the pig's way of life to live like that, but are children pigs? Away with flesh,' she says, 'the minister is quite right when he says the same'—she had just come out of church. —And now she wanted to go out, you say; why didn't you lock her in, Uncle Holtfreter?

HOLTFRETER: *uneasily*] There's the mayor, coming straight towards us: go away, Grüntal, I must have a word with the mayor—Mr. Mayor!

GRÜNTAL *waits.* MAYOR *comes hurriedly round the corner, returns their greeting and continues on his way.*

HOLTFRETER: *calmly blocks his path*] Mr. Mayor, it's not right, you know!

MAYOR: Alright, alright, Mr. . . . Mr. . . . aren't you Mr. Holtfreter, the shoemaker? I have a Council meeting, Mr. Holtfreter.

HOLTFRETER: . . . Not right at all, Mr. Mayor!

MAYOR: Come along with me, Mr. Holtfreter, we're going the same way. I can see you want the police and I'm going to the City Chambers. By the way, did you notice—wasn't that Boll, the land-owner, and his wife just going into that shop together?

I have to have a few words with him.

HOLTFRETER: Boll's shopping, he has the money and he takes his time. Round here they call him Blue Boll.

MAYOR: I know . . . but . . .

HOLTFRETER: But if he loves his life as he does, then he has to look after it as long as he has it. Kindness brings its own reward and if he carries on much longer being as kind to himself as he has been, then his reward will be a big bang, Mr. Mayor, he'll have a stroke, that's what—

MAYOR: I really can't wait until he's finished in there—good-bye, Mr. Holtfreter.

HOLTFRETER: *sternly*] If the Lord Mayor has no time to wait for a land-owner like Boll, then naturally it is hopeless for a simple citizen of this city to try to catch the Lord Mayor's ear, be it the right one or the left.

MAYOR: Oh, you wanted to put something to me, Mr. Holtfreter. Go ahead then—tell me. What is it?

GRÜNTAL *tries to get a word in.*

HOLTFRETER: Be quiet, Grüntal. How can the fact that your wife has left you, interest the Lord Mayor? [*to* MAYOR] You see, he is my brother-in-law and a pig-keeper from Parum, that's all—Mr. Mayor, three or four days ago a gentleman came into my workshop—I live in Grünwinkel.

MAYOR: *resigned*] I see—and then?

HOLTFRETER: . . . comes up the steps, I work over the pig-styes— how shall I describe it, comes hopping or springing or dancing up —something like that. Orders footgear for his right foot, club foot, Mr. Mayor, genuine club foot, if not a cloven hoof—does his ordering—leaves his foot and the whole right leg there, puts his hat on and hops or springs or dances down the steps past the pig-stye—and is gone.

MAYOR: I hereby instruct that the leg be immediately deposited in the Office of the Chief of Police.

HOLTFRETER: The leg? No, no, Mr. Mayor, that's just the point, that's why I am running round the streets here and can't see any order in it. The leg has escaped from my workshop like a leg built for a jolly jig, a well-sprung, unashamedly merry leg, with a real devil of a backside on it—so the leg is galloping around and, Mr. Mayor, you'd better organize beaters to hunt it, otherwise all order is lost.

BOLL *steps out of the shop and nods.*

BOLL: Is it convenient, Mr. Mayor, or—I see you are busy!

MAYOR: Be right with you, Mr. Boll. [*to* HOLTFRETER] I shall have this affair looked into, Mr. Holtfreter, definitely, you can rest assured.

GRÜNTAL: Come alone then, Uncle Holtfreter, the Mayor has had enough of our family affairs. [*both off*].

MAYOR: Now then, Mr. Boll, how is your good lady? and yourself?

BOLL: Oh, so-so . . . Look, thanks very much, Mr. Mayor, but . . .

MAYOR: But . . .

BOLL: What an incredible state of affairs, Mr. Mayor, I pledge you my word and solemnly declare it is gnawing me hollow and scraping me raw inside that this is the way things are and not otherwise. Incredible, Mr. Mayor!

MAYOR: I am really sorry, Mr. Boll, that this is how things are and not otherwise, and especially that I or another branch of the City Council seem to be responsible for it.

BOLL: Certainly, Mr. Mayor, somebody has to get the blame—so you are the one! What hair-raising absurdity!

MAYOR: I am grateful to you from the bottom of my heart for your frankness—but may I ask exactly what you had in mind?

BOLL: *with face swelling up blue*] A damnable and inexcusable, senselessly bungled business, that's what I had in mind. Can senseless bungling be excused, eh? Can a senselessly bungled business be defended? A fine defence that would be!

MAYOR: I hope that nobody will be found to defend something so incontestably questionable, at least not in our town.

BOLL: Bad, bad!

MAYOR: Doubtless, but looking at this regrettable business as a whole, from which aspect of it exactly would you say some blame might attach to me? for my part?

BOLL: Part? There, you see, with me it's all or nothing today— parts here, parts there, let's forget the parts, shall we? Is it all above board, Mr. Mayor? Better alive than dead, that is the heart of the matter. How abominably inappropriate the human creature is in this life—how is he brought into this cow of a life—is he ever asked, 'with your permission'? Cow of a life—what do you mean? Don't we do pretty well? Oh, very well, better, better still and better and better—and suddenly what do I see—it's not going to be better and better, but bad and worse and still worse. What a mean impertinence and—look, Reverend Sir, what a horrible trap snaps after our flesh and bones, with oiled joints and sharp jaws! Wham! and we have to submit. Live well at first, too well, perhaps, and then . . . well, that's how it goes!

MAYOR: I understand entirely, Mr. Boll, you cast one glance at the problem and immediately your great sensitivity leads you off into the widest possible ramifications.

BOLL: How can Boll the land-owner help being Boll the land-owner? He is unasked, simply not-asked whether he wanted to become Boll the land-owner or not. It's really a piece of impertinence, to make Boll the land-owner into Boll the land-owner—for what good does it do him, Reverend Sir? He is his own master and servant at one and the same time, and how can the servant be content with such a master?

MAYOR: Yes, yes.

BOLL: *laughs*] Look out, Mr. Medical Adviser! Remember you said: Boll drinks, Boll gambles, Boll spends all his time sitting around lording it mightily on the majesty of his backside. Boll's enemy is the topsy-turvy life he leads, but he treats it as his greatest friend.

MAYOR: Just as Boll has ridden his strength lame and must now proceed on his weakness.

BOLL: Quite right, Boll has shot his deer and is banging off his gun into the empty forest—to put it in a nutshell: Boll has Boll by the throat, before him nothing but the leanness of his good prospects, before him everything, except what is good, welcome, friendly—nothing but devilish rubbish—he'd better find a way to cope with it? [*offers cigars*] Have a coffin-nail!

MAYOR: *declines*] You too should refrain from heavy smoking, Mr. Boll!

BOLL: What do you mean, should? Shouldn't it be: Boll must?

MAYOR: Mr. Boll, although I have been at the receiving end of this conversation I am quite out of breath. My interest in you . . .

BOLL: Boll is killing Boll—can you stop that?

MAYOR: But perhaps he could stop it himself? Mr. Boll, an impulse of candid cordiality enables me to agree that in effect it is apparently true that Boll is killing Boll; but why, dear sir, is one of these two a harmful Boll—couldn't he be like a good, honourable lawyer who sees to it that Boll secures all the delightful possibilities of the coming years, or who even protects him with shrewd solicitude? Couldn't Boll even be Boll's own best helper?

BOLL: Here's my wife, Mr. Mayor, let's leave Boll to himself; and let him find a way, as I have, I believe, already said.

MAYOR: The City Councillors are waiting—meeting at eleven o'clock on the dot, Mr. Boll. I take my leave. [*off.*]

MRS. BOLL: *coming out of the shop*] We've hardly been half an hour. Kurt, do you hear me?

BOLL *looks at his watch, nods.*

MRS. BOLL: And right from the start there's no end to the rush. I'm sure it couldn't have been all that time already—or what do you think?

BOLL: I'm going over to Grotappel's for an hour or two: you coming?

MRS. BOLL: I don't know what to make of you, Kurt!

BOLL: Oh, I must have a few drinks to give me courage. The do with the Prunkhorsts will go on and on—so Dutch courage! You know, it's lucky that I at least have the heart for it. Anybody who has so many festive years behind him should be allowed to stop and get drunk on total abstinence.

MRS. BOLL: *taken aback*] Well, how shall I have any peace of mind to do my errands if I must continually be thinking . . . what did you mean, really, when you suddenly said yesterday evening like a shot from a gun: 'Everybody is his own best neighbour! especially on an estate where there are no neighbours for miles around'—or something like that. 'Not me,' you said then, 'I should not like to be somebody like that.' You can see for yourself it's enough to give anyone a start! First of all you are clearly speaking about yourself, then you say, 'I shouldn't like to be in his skin'— what on earth is that supposed to mean?

BOLL: Not one bit, I shouldn't like that one little bit, not one little bit!

MRS. BOLL: You make me quite dizzy, for what kind of an answer is that! I'd honestly like to know how you always manage to find new ways of torturing me.

BOLL: That's good, couldn't possibly be better.

MRS. BOLL: Who? What?

BOLL: Look, Martha, how the tower climbs and climbs, and then climbs no more. But in the mist it has such a hazy perspective that you think it is playing a little joke with its spire, pressing upwards out of sight—I feel good like it does, for I am convinced it feels good.

MRS. BOLL: Kurt, I'm so easily frightened—didn't you feel one of your stupid dizzy spells, haven't you perhaps got a touch of blood pressure again?

BOLL: Why should I—why should I have anything to do with something like that, of all things?

MRS. BOLL: Oh, God, there's another example, what kind of answer is that, it's enough to give one funny ideas.

VIRGIN *the watchmaker goes past, unlocks the church door, goes in, leaving the door ajar. Both give him a brief glance.*

BOLL: The funniest idea is that in many cases you can't tell for sure whether the idea is funny or normal. For instance!

MRS. BOLL: Oh stop, Kurt, I have still so much shopping to do. Now then, Kurt . . . where did I put my list, can't you help me find it . . . ah, here it is, thank goodness! Now Kurt, four o'clock at the latest at the 'Golden Orb' for a meal? [*she puts a screeching stress on the word 'meal'*] The Prunkhorsts are sure to be there at three, remember, now I really must. . . . [*off*].

BOLL: Remember? Of course, but not the way you think. [*looks up in the air*] The air is heavy with it, the air brings it, the air delivers it up—[*laughs*] Haven't felt so well for a long time. Dizzy spell? I'd a feeling somebody mentioned dizzy spells?—Did somebody mention dizzy spells?

GRETA GRÜNTAL *in Sunday best, a bright kerchief over her head, appears and looks boldly into* BOLL'S *eyes as she passes.* BOLL *puts his hand in his breast pocket and pulls out his cigar case, selects a long, fat cigar and lights it, while he follows* GRETA *with his eyes.*

BOLL: *looks around*] That way to my Medical Adviser . . . so about turn, march! [*turns about and prepares to follow* GRETA, *when she comes hurrying back and passes quickly. She is followed by* GRÜNTAL *who puts a hand on her shoulder*].

GRÜNTAL: You've been out walking a bit long, haven't you, Greta? [GRETA *tries to go on, so he puts his other hand on her and turns her round*].

GRÜNTAL: To Parum, Greta, you've surely forgotten we're going to Parum, and this is the way, Greta—straight ahead.

BOLL *pushes him to one side, he turns round, they look at each other,* GRETA *slips into the shop.*

GRÜNTAL: Well, sir—or whatever you are!

BOLL: *waves his cigar]* Hands off, understand, hands off the woman, that's all.

GRÜNTAL: But she's my own wife!

BOLL: Exactly, exactly—just keep your hands off her, *because* she's your own wife!

GRÜNTAL *looks around, leaves* BOLL *and runs round the nearest corner.* GRETA *comes out, looks at him questioningly.*

BOLL: *points with his cigar]* Mm—somebody looking for you.

GRETA: Can I hide anywhere?

BOLL: *points to the church door]* The tower is open—just have to lean on the door. [GRETA *slips in at the portal].*

GRÜNTAL [*back*] Where is she, where can she be?

BOLL *points in the opposite direction.* GRÜNTAL *runs off.*

BOLL [*throws the cigar away*] Can't accept responsibility for everything. If she absolutely insists on burning away, then she'll have to find another smoker. Now then, not going to the doctor is a matter of principle, not going to Grottappel a matter of prudence —but to the tower, yes, to the tower! [*off into the tower].*

2

Narrow room half-way up the tower. At the back one can see the darkness of the church roof, on the left the narrow spiral staircase comes in from below, on the right in the wall it continues upwards. A Gothic window. Slow ticking of the clock seems to penetrate across the space and through the walls. Greta is sitting on the threshold to the attic room. Boll climbs up from below, breathing heavily.

GRETA: Are you somebody?

BOLL: No—never been anybody—I'm nobody!—

GRETA: Are you somebody, I asked, and have you any say here?

BOLL: *points to the window]* Your husband is standing down below there studying all the corners, only place he hasn't looked is up here, never enters his head—have you any children?

GRETA *withdraws even more into herself. Pause.*

GRETA: *grumbling*] All suffocating in flesh—you too—in flesh.

BOLL: Let's forget flesh, away with flesh—look, woman, apart from my flesh I am something else entirely, like something towering up, like a tower, something quite decidedly different.

GRETA: Have you any say here, do you belong here?

BOLL: I stay where it suits me, I feel good here and here I stay.

GRETA: Shall I go back down?

BOLL: As long as it suits you, stay here too.

GRETA: And where am I to go, anyway!

BOLL: If you have children, why don't you go to your children— flesh to flesh, tower to tower—I'm staying.

GRETA *gets up.*

BOLL: Your husband is still down there, he'll beat you.

GRETA: He has never done that, never will, I'm not afraid of him— but he will take me back to the children.

BOLL: Is that bad? If so, who for?

GRETA: The poor souls . . .

BOLL: Go on, tell me about it.

GRETA: Their poor souls whisper and cry to me to be let out and they're begging, begging, all the time, want to get out and moan that it's through me they are in misery—misery, they call it.

BOLL: Their poor souls whisper?

GRETA: They call out and scream—I hear it most clearly in the dark when everybody's asleep.

BOLL: And have they anything to cry about?

GRETA: *flatly*] Their poor souls cry out, the growing flesh chokes their voices, but their poor souls keep tormenting me to free them from the flesh.

BOLL: How many of them are there all told?

GRETA: Three souls I have brought into the cursed flesh.

BOLL: I too am just such a poor soul.

GRETA: Yes, I know, but why did you talk about a tower?

BOLL. I feel better when I lie—you see, with lies I chastise my flesh, with lies I hack my flesh into a thousand pieces and throw the shreds to the dogs—and then, scarcely have the dogs fallen on the thousand shreds, when there is a flash of lightning which moves a bit here and a bit there and it's whole again. The air is heavy with it, the air fetches it, the air delivers it up—am I myself again, or am I not myself any more, or have I never been myself at all?

My blood is red, but it makes me go blue in the face. Who are you anyway?

GRETA: At home in the village they call me the witch—don't know why. I have my thoughts and if dying comes into the question then it's probably not worse than being alive.

BOLL: I have always lived well and according to a damnably strict order of things I must die badly. I wish I could begin to acquire a taste for death. But as it is, because I am as I am, I must be afraid—and I don't like waiting for dying.

GRETA: Anyone no longer in the flesh is fortunate—and I must release my children from the flesh.

BOLL: *breathing heavily looks at her, turns to the window, and looks out. Then he approaches hesitantly and unsteadily, puts his hand in his breastpocket and takes out his cigar-case, pushes it back again immediately —then stretching out his arms seems to fall on* GRETA. *She pushes her hands against his chest and holds him back*] Don't choke me, it will be alright—something pressed me down, I felt something, and I just had to hold on to you. [*he goes back and leans against the wall*].

GRETA: Should I fetch somebody? [BOLL *shakes his head and closes his eyes*] You'd be better off in bed.

BOLL: *forces his eyes wide open*] I am on my feet, what do I have my long legs for? Don't want to lie down, just hold me tight a minute! [GRETA *supports him*] Does me good, when you touch me, I knew that, that's why I groped my way over to you, when everything went black before my eyes. [*composed again*] Dear old flesh! Can't give that up. [*thoughtfully*] What happened then? Did I bang my nose on the corner at the crossways, banged it and lost my direction for a second, got confused? Anyway I came out of it alright and here I am again on the old familiar path.

VIRGIN *the clockmaker comes down the steps from above.*

VIRGIN: My God—am I seeing right—Mr. Boll? [GRETA *lets* BOLL *go, but remains standing beside him*].

BOLL: Not that I know of. [*to* GRETA] What an excitable fellow!

VIRGIN: My name is Virgin—Virgin the watchmaker.

BOLL: An exceptionally lovely name.

VIRGIN: As lovely, if not lovelier than yours, Mr. Boll.

BOLL: Boll? You'd better ask somewhere else if there is anybody of that name here.

VIRGIN: So you're not Boll. Well, you ought to know. Anyway

please excuse me for confusing you with that gentleman, it is not exactly complimentary.

BOLL: And what is he like, this Mr. Boll, if I may ask?

VIRGIN: I believe he thinks himself a kind of non-pareil in every sense, does Mr. Boll.

BOLL: So, then clearly a man to be envied.

VIRGIN: The blasted works of the clock tower were jammed again— so there I was up there wasting my time like Boll, Mr. Boll, does his . . .

BOLL: The same Mr. Boll?

VIRGIN: The very same, what else is there for a man like him to do except let his time go to waste down the drain. I'm not speaking too quietly, am I? I am a bit narrow-chested and what with going up and down these stairs, well—you see what I mean?

BOLL: Don't you worry.

VIRGIN: Well, what I really wanted to tell you . . .

BOLL: Still on the subject of Boll, I hope?

VIRGIN: Naturally, but maybe you have already heard about it somewhere else, the business of Boll and Count Ravenklau?

BOLL: Ravenklau—Ravenklau?

VIRGIN: Count von Ravenklau etc., you know, the Patron of our new Apostolic Brotherhood—I belong to it too, so . . .

BOLL: I understand—

VIRGIN: Well, the Count had several times spoken in public, un-fortunately not without thereby giving occasion to all sorts of ill-feeling.

BOLL: I have a vague recollection—there was far more talk about the Count than all his public speeches merited.

VIRGIN: *starts*] Hm-yes, as you will. More than anybody else, Boll had, as he boasted, made things hot for the whole apostolic brood, and—if you'll pardon me—deeply wounded this noble and good old gentleman. So, what happened?

BOLL: I'm really dying to know.

VIRGIN: *gesticulating*] Just listen: at the Annual Races in our city last year, after the first race, Mr. Boll comes from the other side straight across the turf towards the stand, which is the kind of thing only Boll would dare to do. Like this—see! Sails along crammed full of his own self-esteem, fresh from the incense of his own self-adulation, a triumphal procession all to himself. The sun sparkles on his face and his legs—every step an earthquake, magnificent. Now as fate would have it, Count Ravenklau is obliged to take the self-same path and walks towards him.

BOLL: Had something to do at the other side presumably?

VIRGIN: Naturally—they move towards each other and the whole stand holds its breath. The Count, short-sighted as he is, is only a few steps away from Boll when he becomes aware of him and turns round, turns his back on him and heads for his seat—yes, that's how it was.

BOLL: Not very exciting so far, Mr. Virgin.

VIRGIN: But think of Boll, dear sir, what was there left for Boll to do—could he continue on his way and so be forced to follow the Count, who had just cut him in public. Escort the Count as it were submissively like a dog, three steps behind, docilely and politely—docile, sir—could he? He did just that—but . . .

BOLL: Well?

VIRGIN: But how, sir, how! The sun which before had been glistening on his face became chilly, the splendour of his countenance disintegrated, Boll's face, the swollen bloom of the festivities, coloured and became plunged in inky shadows of shame. He took it, sir, what do you say to that?

BOLL: What is there to say? I wish I could have seen it from the stand.

VIRGIN: You'd have witnessed a once-in-a-blue-moon.

BOLL: I am not as surprised as you are that Boll took it—perhaps he is not so crammed full of self-esteem as you think—but he took it! The old gentleman had probably given the Apostolic Brotherhood some pretty good pointers.

VIRGIN: Pointers, dear sir? He had spoken of the fact that man is in a state of becoming, not being, he had discussed that, you call that pointers? Our being, he had said, is a mere spring, but our life a stream of becoming with no goal but that of becoming, constantly renewed. That's what he said—eternal becoming! To-day is but a mean to-morrow, to-morrow is superseded by the day after. I suppose you've never—you've probably never, no never, heard a word about such things?

BOLL: Me? I thought we were talking about Boll?

VIRGIN: Law, compulsion, inescapability—well, I really must be going, Mr. Boll.

BOLL: Say hello to Mr. Boll for me when you see him and tell him to look me up, I'll make him believe in this business of to-morrow and the day after—watch you don't fall climbing down.

VIRGIN: *hesitates*] For how long, if I may ask, do you intend to view the tower—I'm only asking.

BOLL: You can leave the key with me, it will be returned to you in due course.

VIRGIN: *hands over the key*] Very good, Mr. Boll. [*to* GRETA] What are you doing here?

GRETA, *embarrassed, gazes into a corner.*

BOLL: No need to ask, Mr. Virgin.

VIRGIN: Well, Mr. Boll, if you will be reponsible for the woman . . .

BOLL: That's alright, I will, I take full responsibility.

VIRGIN: Then I'm quite happy. [*climbs down*].

BOLL: He's learned his catechism very well—how did it go again: Eternal becoming? Very pretty, it reminds me what passable music can be made with simple instruments, with a mouth organ, for instance—well, we're still standing here, can't even sit down— let's look out a little. [*looks out the window*] God, this Sternberg, what a rubbish-heap, a mere handful of a place! You go round to the right to Grotappel's—down here so directly underneath you could spit on it, is the roof of the 'Golden Orb'—aha, and there goes Monsieur Virgin, look, child, a black spot moving across the market-place, you can't see the narrow chest from here, but you can see the bent back . . .

GRETA *suddenly puts her arms round his neck.*

BOLL: Heh, heh, what's this, what's the matter?

GRETA: You are Mr. Boll, aren't you?

BOLL: Did you doubt it for a minute?

GRETA: I want to ask Mr. Boll for something.

BOLL: Ask for something? Splendid, my child, ask!

GRETA: Mr. Boll can get it, he can, he must.

BOLL: Get it—well I can get it if it's possible. What's it to be, then?

GRETA: *still holding him tightly; gently*] What's needed— . . . people call it poison.

BOLL: Poison—but surely not for the children? [GRETA *nods and makes some incomprehensible reply in a choking voice*].

BOLL: *tries to free himself*] So—so that your children can die, you want me to . . .

GRETA: You must! [*pressing hard against him*].

BOLL: Are you clear in your own mind about this?

GRETA: You must!

BOLL: Oho—Boll must?

GRETA: Yes, you must do it, so that it is done without any moaning, without torment—and—[*she presses closer*]—It must be all over before I am out the door.

BOLL: Of course, I understand, a few white crumbs or something on the end of a spoon.

GRETA: As long as it's quick.

BOLL: *tries to free himself*] I'll consider it, child, just be satisfied with the fact that I promise to think about it.

GRETA: *holds him tight*] You're to promise and do it, no need to think about it.

BOLL: How can I promise, when I don't even know whom I should see about it—and what shall I say, and just what kind of story do I make up to ask for it?

GRETA: Mr. Boll has promised and agreed to get it.

BOLL: Just tell me one thing: what will you do when you are out the door and you can say it is finished?

GRETA: *lets him go, looks at him amazed and incredulous*] I—I—I—? [*stammering*] It is finished?

BOLL: Yes, of course—you must realize you'll be arrested.

GRETA: When it is finished—[*twines her arms round his neck, sobbing*]— I shall do nothing but give thanks, thanks.

BOLL: Well, we haven't reached that stage yet.

GRETA: Oh yes, now it is as good as done. Finished: you can get it by this evening.

BOLL: Listen, child—what is your first name anyway?

GRETA: I'm Greta.

BOLL: Well, then, Greta, my dear witch, what's to happen to me afterwards, have you thought of that—after all I'll have been involved in it too.

GRETA: *lets him go, goes slowly to the steps*] You, you let yourself be insulted by the Count, go and take your disgrace for a walk. You're no good—Boll must, you say, but you don't mean it.

BOLL: *holds her back*] And what if I do bring what you need?

GRETA: So that it can be finished?

BOLL: Easily and quickly and surely finished, then it is finished!

GRETA: *looks at him half-smiling, lays her hands lightly on his*] Bring it this evening!

BOLL: Will you love me for it if I do?

GRETA: Yes, if you have done it by this evening—yes, for that—yes, then I would!

BOLL: This evening . . .

GRETA: *trembling*] Where?

BOLL: After dark in Cathedral Street.

GRETA: After dark, without fail after dark in Cathedral Street.

BOLL: We'll meet there.

GRETA: Then you'll have it.

BOLL: I hope I'll have it by then.

GRETA: By then he'll have it!

3

Street. Holtfreter with several citizens.

HOLTFRETER: . . . well, believe me or believe me not: hop, hop, down the steps it went, hopping, dancing, springing with a real devil of a backside on it—believe me or believe me not!

1ST CITIZEN: Did you see this yourself—I mean with your very own eyes?

HOLTFRETER: Do you think I am running about the streets just for exercise? Don't I have to work for a living, eh? Am I well-known as an honourable man, or not? Am I not on my feet all day and every day with no thought for anything but work?

GRÜNTAL *comes round the corner.*

HOLTFRETER: Is it possible, Grüntal—still in Sternberg? You haven't seen the leg anywhere on your travels, have you?

GRÜNTAL: You haven't come across Greta?

HOLTFRETER: Oh yes—Greta! No-o—what would she be doing here—she'll be back in Parum long since.

GRÜNTAL: What about your leg, Uncle Holtfreter, that devil of a leg? I suppose it's back in the workshop too, long since, squatting on its one cheek—do you imagine it will let the Sternberg dogs hunt it all morning?

They go off and stand nearby. Enter MRS. BOLL, *followed by* SAUGWURM
the coachman, who is laden with parcels.

MRS. BOLL: He hasn't been to the doctor either, and Grotappel
hasn't seen him—take a run round and look in at Ohl's,
Saugwurm, will you? And say the Prunkhorsts have been there
for ages—and want to eat as soon as possible, you know. First
on the left along Hangman's Alley, you know.

SAUGWORM *off.* BOLL *appears from the other side.*

BOLL: Ah, there you are Martha—waiting for somebody?

MRS. BOLL: Really, Kurt, I have been asking for you everywhere—
and you're nowhere; where's a body to look if you're not
anywhere?

BOLL: If I am nowhere, then I don't exist at all, Martha—just got
lost, that's all.

MAYOR *comes.*

MAYOR: Ah, Mr. Boll, we meet again—how fortunate! . . . Good-
day, Madame, could you be patient for just a second? We
business-men, you know how it is—and all that.

MRS. BOLL: Gladly—as long as you don't deprive him of his meal,
Mr. Mayor, and me and the others too—you may borrow him,
but on the understanding that we must eat.

MAYOR: Oh, just one small item—I've just remembered—so, Mr.
Boll, something I shouldn't have forgotten this morning, the
agreement about the bull must be settled as soon as possible.
[*meanwhile* GRÜNTAL *approaches slowly, keeping his eye on* BOLL]
If you would communicate with the man from the Grazing
Deputation, or even Councillor Nuszboom, either by letter . . .
or of course better still would be if you got in touch with him
personally . . .

GRÜNTAL: *to* BOLL] Excuse me, sir, I'd almost wager you are the
same man . . .

BOLL: Of course, Mayor, I should just like to ask you . . . perhaps
you'll allow me to accompany you to the next corner. [*go off
together;* GRÜNTAL *follows*] I might just possibly manage to look
Nuszboom up in his office today. [*to* GRÜNTAL] Alright, alright,
your turn later—I'm busy at the moment. Well then, Mr. Mayor!

MAYOR: Yes, that would be best, I am extremely pleased . . . [*to*
GRÜNTAL] My good man, don't be so impatient!

GRÜNTAL: Don't worry about that—I have other things in my head.

Impatience can wait.

MAYOR: Anyway I can assure you, you won't get very far if you adopt that tone. [*to* BOLL] I'll just come back with you to take my leave of your wife, Mr. Boll.

GRÜNTAL *turns back too and walks alongside the* Mayor.

MAYOR: *stops*] Now look here—I must say—I find this a bit much.

GRÜNTAL: *stops too*] I can take a hint. Alright, I have to wait—I'll do my best to see that it's done with all speed, that I can promise you boldly and yet in all deference.

MAYOR: *to* BOLL] Do you understand what's going on, Mr. Boll? [*to* GRÜNTAL] What do you want of us anyway?

GRÜNTAL: Well, if you're ready now, I can start. [*to* BOLL] I want to ask the gentleman for some information. Where the answers are, is where you have to ask.

BOLL: Information—answer—who are you anyway?

GRÜNTAL: I knew right from the start you just have to be polite with the gentleman then you can wind him round your little finger. But I should just like to make it clear to the gentleman that I don't want to keep him, not for anything in the world—and if the gentleman would not beat about the bush so much . . .

BOLL: *to* MAYOR] The fellow has been wandering the streets for ages —I'll settle this little business afterwards on my own—Martha, the Mayor would like to say good-bye.

MRS. BOLL *approaches,* GRÜNTAL *slips in front of her.*

GRÜNTAL: The business with my wife comes first, the gentleman knows what I mean.

BOLL *pushes him away,* GRÜNTAL *clutches the* MAYOR's *arm firmly.*

MAYOR: You're palpably molesting me—let go!

GRÜNTAL: *lets go*] It's not so much that, I've maybe even touched you with my dirty hands. [*tapping him on the shoulder*] You see my hands are dirty and if I've palpably got you dirty, then I'll palpably make you clean again, as is right and proper. This gentleman here isn't so particular about such things.

MRS. BOLL: For heaven's sake, Kurt, let's go! [*to* MAYOR] I'm afraid he might strike him dead on the spot.

GRÜNTAL: Just keep calm, Madame. If you mean by that, that he might kill me, then I can easily put you right. The only thing he wants to do is to tell me where he spent his time with my wife, that's all.

MRS. BOLL: You dare say that in broad daylight on a public thoroughfare?

GRÜNTAL: The business with my wife was also on a public thoroughfare, though it was early this morning. I can remember quite clearly that it was my wife and no other.

BOLL: . . . still that was rather a long time ago! [to MRS. BOLL] He was guilty of somewhat unseemly behaviour, you know—and I reprimanded him for it.

GRÜNTAL: That's quite true as far as it goes, but then where did you hide with my wife?

BOLL: Get somebody else to tell you.

MRS. BOLL: Kurt!

BOLL: The affair isn't worthy of your attention—keep out of it, not worth while. But listen, you know what I was thinking when I was coming round the corner earlier, something really worth telling: supposing the old ladies up there on the tower suddenly stand up and blast away at us with their trumpets . . .

MRS. BOLL: My God, Kurt. Where do you get all these crazy ideas? What old ladies?

BOLL: You know, the angels—who are to rouse in dread all the deaf dead from their graves on Judgment Day. Oh, what a rage of howling and screaming would start then on the market-place, I thought to myself, God in Heaven, the cry wouldn't be 'The meal, the meal'—the cry would be 'Don't plead putrefaction—everybody up!' Lucky those who can say then: 'Why do you ask me, I am somebody different!' See to it, my children, see to it that you become different, so they can't ask you! [to MRS. BOLL] Just imagine, we won't even be able to drive up in the coach and you won't have any jewellery and finery, maybe you won't even have a shift to put on.

GRÜNTAL: In Madame's case, no-one will doubt that Madame can, with God's blessing, allow herself to be seen even without a shift.

BOLL: Let it pass—still time, and in the end probably a shift will be necessary.

MRS. BOLL: I just keep asking myself how you can let that man get away with it—how can he dare in your presence and mine! Just tell me one thing: what do you intend to do about it?

BOLL: Do about it, we'll just let that pass, where would that lead us—no, children, listen: why do you ask me, I am somebody different and you speak of doing something about it?

MRS. BOLL: *to* MAYOR] Don't you find that downright queer?

MAYOR: Mr. Boll, Mr. Boll.

BOLL: Mr. Boll. So I am Boll and no other. There's the rub, no peace from yourself for a minute. You see, Martha, no matter what I do—Boll stays Boll—the more I deny Boll, the more obviously exposed do I stand there, naked and exposed, even my shift is becoming suspect, no, Martha, it just cannot be, no hiding-place far and wide, not even in one's shift. Boll, nothing but Boll!

GRÜNTAL: You see, Madame, he is ready to answer for it, if he has been up to something somewhere. None of us can get round that, one can count on it. And so one can count on Boll, even with your gracious presence one can count on him as much as if you weren't here. [*laughs*].

BOLL: My wife and I can manage quite well without your approval, just bear that in mind! Let's have some respect, and hold your tongue!

GRÜNTAL: Just like that—in the twinkling of an eye—you see, that kind of respect wants to be able to take things easy and scratch its backside in peace now and again. Maybe your wife has a clean shift on her body, but my wife Greta certainly has one on . . .

MRS. BOLL: Say something, Mr. Mayor, after all it is my own husband!

MAYOR: Only too gladly, madame, I'm only afraid I might anticipate your husband.

BOLL: We'll soon settle all this. [*to* GRÜNTAL] Look, man, what's on your mind anyway! Respect, respect, your cheek is almost enough to inspire some! Where do you get the cheek? Martha, don't you find something like respect growing on you, too?

MRS. BOLL: My only reply to that can be no reply, Kurt. I am ashamed for you, but I am ashamed in silence, and summon up my pride to assist me. Look, it's because I have pride enough for you too, that I manage to be ashamed in silence. You see what I mean?

BOLL: But, Martha, what tinpot reasons cloud your sky. [*to* MAYOR] Am I already so much somebody else that I do not recognize my own wife? Proud and silent?

MAYOR: Be that as it may, your wife's reasons for pride and silence are nevertheless . . .

BOLL: But the man is a perfectly honest fellow, Mr. Mayor: in short he is in the right. Naturally my wife can't help the fact that he is in the right—no, Martha, stop that business with your lower lip, don't do that—you have summoned up pride and silence and there is nothing better, so you're right again as always.

MAYOR: With that this unedifying interlude has come to a close—madame, I herewith return the devoted husband appertaining to you. [to BOLL] Besides I am no doubt right in assuming that it's a question of something purely private?

BOLL: Absolutely, Mr. Mayor.

MAYOR: Well, then—Madame!

BOLL: to GRÜNTAL] Are you still there? But we're quits! You are right, I'll give it to you in writing. And with that in your pocket you can go and get lost.

GRÜNTAL: As you have conferred so many riches on me, I shouldn't like to depart with ingratitude, sir, so be good enough to add the last little detail.

BOLL: If I think back, I have a feeling your wife is called Greta—or isn't she?

GRÜNTAL: You can't change it. Greta's her name and Greta's always been her name. And Greta has often 'gone off' like this before—but so far she's always got better again. The doctor says it doesn't mean a thing, he says. Afterwards she is pretty peevish, but then, then the good times come back to our place, and Greta is the jolliest woman in the world.

BOLL: You know you're not the only one? Oh, God—what do you think—we've all got some bridle or other stuck into our mouths, to chew on, and it's free of charge—but the bridle is there, there's no changing that.

GRÜNTAL: Yes, Mr. Boll, you are a great man to have a yarn with, and as for the bridle, that can be taken out. And if the whole street round about is prepared to stand on its head, then I'll take the bit out of my mouth and put it between your teeth. Then you can champ on it and it's yours, free of charge—but it is the responsibility for Greta you are biting on, you can't get away from that.

BOLL: Responsibility? That doesn't suit me at all at the moment—must that be?

GRÜNTAL: Well, sir, you must know that for yourself, if you stop to think. All the ladies and gentlemen are witnesses, that I have placed the harness on you and I can congratulate you on how well it suits you.

MAYOR: Watch out, Mr. Boll, for God's and Mrs. Boll's sake, hesitate before you accept— . . . I . . . I know . . .

BOLL: And so do I, Mr. Mayor, I know all about it, but we are not of the same opinion. [to MRS. BOLL] What I thought was this Martha—you go on ahead to the 'Golden Orb' and have them serve. As for Otto—stick the wine list into his hand and tell him to open at page three, top right, where there are half-a-dozen or so stinkers of French names and he can pick out the most unpronounceable. [looks at his watch] Yes, he's a great fellow to have a yarn with. I have just one more little errand. [grabs his belly] Must take precautions for all eventualities, which may or may not come up after the meal—a few pennyworth of white crumbs or something for the end of a spoon. [to MRS. BOLL] Just have to make one little call at the chemist's. Mr. Mayor! [off].

MAYOR and MRS. BOLL look at each other.

HOLTFRETER: over to GRÜNTAL] You're pretty quick to attach yourself to the cream of society, Grüntal, now you must let me have a word with the mayor as well. It's certainly not your fault if your arrangements haven't helped, but where do we go from here?

MAYOR: Oh, God, Holtfreter, things don't move so quickly, you know.

HOLTFRETER: There's no question of things moving quickly, on the contrary it's slow, slow and couldn't be slower.

GRÜNTAL: pulls him away] Can't you see, Uncle Holtfreter, the mayor can't make any arrangements, because you won't leave him alone to make any. [both off].

MAYOR: Really, Mrs. Boll, what an admirable woman you are, Mrs. Boll! What astonishing self-control in the face of such regrettable seizures—attacks of forgetfulness—self-forgetfulness—on your husband's part!

MRS. BOLL: You've found the right word for its straightaway, Mr. Mayor—forgetfulness—you see he literally forgets who he is.

MAYOR: One might even call him lost.

MRS. BOLL: As if he had lost himself, often I don't know any more— he's completely lost all feelings for what's right and proper . . .

yes, you know he once said, 'Child,' he said to me, 'you are a
wonderful wife, that's as constant as Judgment Day, you be
content with that, be happy: a wonderful wife!' 'But then, if
you admit that,' I said . . . 'No buts,' he shouts at me, 'no buts,
a wonderful wife, that's a lot, a great deal, and indeed nobody
dares to doubt it . . . well, then!'

MAYOR: He . . . well, Mrs. Boll . . .

MRS. BOLL: What do you think?

MAYOR: Well, look at it this way, we were speaking of how he has
lost himself, shouldn't one approach the question carefully and
say that the lost one, as it were the Boll-to-date, was the wrong
one, while the present and new, newly-found Boll is the true
one—I think the possibility is at least worth thinking about.

MRS. BOLL: Are you serious—that would be ghastly, wouldn't it?

MAYOR: As early as this morning the conversation I had with your
husband left me with . . .

MRS. BOLL: pleading] No, Mr. Mayor, I cannot thank you for such a
disclosure, what an idea, and where does that leave me, if Boll,
my good old Kurt is not the same old Kurt at all!

MAYOR: Many an event brews imperceptibly in the dark depths of
personal experience.

MRS. BOLL: No, but that's, that's unnatural. If this turned out to be
true, it would be an emergency, a tragedy—I should much rather
see him in his grave, for then I should still know who he is,
lying there, who he was and how I could picture him in my mind
for ever and ever—but this way—oh, God!

MAYOR: Mrs. Boll, I deeply regret having indicated such quite
remote possibilties—no, oh, no, basically your husband is without
a doubt fully and completely his old honest self.

MRS. BOLL: Do you really think so, Mr. Mayor? Yes, he is, Kurt is,
isn't he . . . but you must admit that of late now and again . . . I
don't mean he is somebody different entirely, only that he is not
basically, as you yourself said, the good old Kurt, he really is,
always has been and always will be. [weeping] Oh, dear God, I worry
almost too much about him, and you just said exactly what the
old milk-hand, Nierkant, said recently at Krönkhagen in almost
the same words. Our French governess passed it on to me. Now
I really must be quick and be off to the meal—we've already kept

them waiting for ages, a very important engagement! Good-bye, Mr. Mayor. I am quite stiff with hunger.

MAYOR: Madame!

4

Dark street. From behind window shutters left a game of skittles can be heard, and thin singing from the house opposite. In the background over roofs the silhouette of the Cathedral. Greta comes from back, looks about her and disappears into the darkness of a corner of the wall, Boll from front, turns round and stands still. Greta emerges from the shadow and steps up to him from behind.

BOLL: *turns round with a start and passes his hand over her face*] Is it you? [GRETA *remains silent*].

BOLL: But you will give me your hand, Greta! [GRETA *stretches out her hand*] You have a good hand, what a power of healing there is in you, I feel better when you stretch out a little of your warmth like this. Do you realize that, you're good for me, witch?

GRETA: I can't feel anything—is it in your pocket? [*she puts her hand in his coat pocket*] Where is it?

BOLL: I didn't manage to speak to him, it's not to be.

GRETA: If you've nothing to bring, why did you bother to come?

BOLL: You help me, Greta, you help me, even if you hardly want to. If you wanted . . .

GRETA: I only want to if you help me.

BOLL: It is easier for me to speak when I hold your hand— —so let me have it; you want me to explain, don't you? [GRETA *gives her hand*] Look, child, an errand like that is easy—say a few words, hand over a few coppers, as easy as winking, and it's done. But you have to know how to get the message across properly, and it didn't come off—I couldn't find the little corner where I could get the manager by himself for a quiet minute, just the two of us.

GRETA: But you said yourself: Boll must!

BOLL: And then they hunted me, all those who are related to me! Just picture the situation—a man like me in a small town like this— it's like an ox in an open field trying to get into a mouse-hole, so I have gone to the most impossible lengths to keep myself out of sight, have slaved away all afternoon avoiding all the normal occupations of my class—keep that in mind, Greta.

GRETA: It's always keep something in mind—when you know I must and you must.

BOLL: You know, child, I don't believe the point has been reached where Boll must. And I don't believe that you must.

GRETA: Let me go.

BOLL: Not so quickly—this is like in the tower, where I feel good, there I stay—and I feel good with you.

GRETA: Ugh, how well you feel in the flesh—my husband and I know what there is in flesh, and you have much too much—let go.

BOLL: *releases her*] Where do you have to go so quickly, slow down, Greta, and let us talk of something pleasant.

GRETA: Do you think I escaped here from the village, to find flesh? I'm looking for what I need, away with flesh! [*looks about her*] There are too many people here anyway.

BOLL: People—what kind of people?

GRETA: *points*] They were standing outside the windows a minute ago, now you can't see anybody—whether they're there or not, they're people.

BOLL: These are fat shadows, Greta, fatter than even the fattest people can make.

GRETA: But I tell you I saw them! I'm not staying where there are so many people.

BOLL: You know I wanted to help you!

GRETA: I'm going and I'll keep going until I have what I'm looking for. There'll be many a one who'll be more use than you are. It's only your voice I like and it said something about when it is finished.

BOLL: Doesn't my voice come from my flesh?

GRETA: Your voice comes from the good world and you are probably from the good world, but ugh! your flesh! [*she goes down the street and disappears in the dark;* BOLL *accompanies her unnoticed. The door left is opened, a powerful beam of light shines out forming a bright space right across the street.* ELIAS *leans half-out and listens to the hymn from across the way*].

ELIAS: Sounds like a coffee-grinder today, old Croaker Unk must be there—her throat's like a rusty rat-trap and the poor Hallelujah gets pretty well squeezed to death in it.

VOICE: *from inside the inn*] I thought maybe to-day there would not be the usual hymns to disturb the peace and they would auction the good Count's chamber pot instead.

ELIAS: I think it's time—we'll make everything ready, maybe there'll be something in the way of alms for us out of the credit in heaven they are building up over there.

ELIAS *and his* CUSTOMERS *meanwhile carry a table and chairs into the strip of light in the street, so that the group is brilliantly lit.* ELIAS *brings glasses.*

1ST CUSTOMER: Yes, or maybe we'll get the groat that was lost and found, who knows?

2ND CUSTOMER: Can you tell me who the man with the jaw-bone of an ass was?

3RD CUSTOMER: A human monster! We never had to memorize the horrible bits, so it's no use your asking.

1ST CUSTOMER: Be quiet, they're coming. [*the door opposite opens and the sect crumbles away into the darkness*].

ELIAS: Number One exercised restraint and praised somebody else instead of himself. Number Two shouted Hallelujah so loud he gave himself a rupture and bespattered his waistcoast with excess zeal. Number Three—oho—Number Three! Nobody can compete with his nerve. Stick his nose in his own droppings and he says: 'I am anointed; I am anointed!' Number Four, you are only Number Four, but you help Number Five. Add Nothing to Little and you get Something. Number Six, on your feet, you lot, and honour Number Six, long live Auntie Unk. [*they stand up*] Here, Auntie Unk, step back this way, there are people here who appreciate your kind of music. The Devil's Komfy Kitchen, this place is called, give yourself a rest, come on, sit down and let the chair kiss your pious backside.

MRS. UNK: *walking away*] You can't offend me, sir—but do you know that it is written: withdraw to your little chamber and lock out the rest of the world?

ELIAS: I have already done that, I only need to go to my little chamber once a day. [*laughter.* MRS. UNK *hurriedly off.* HOLTFRETER *with the* GENTLEMAN].

HOLTFRETER: Don't hold it against me, sir, that I won't leave you alone—but I couldn't bring myself to do that, sir.

GENTLEMAN: Yes, I can see you want to get acquainted, shall we take a seat here?

HOLTFRETER: Delighted, if you really don't hold it against me. [*they sit*] I have been running around all day and my legs are tired—you don't walk very quickly either, sir.

GENTLEMAN: Just a bit stiff on my feet, this one leg here is not as good as the other.

HOLTFRETER: Yes, I see that, noticed that right away. Have you—are you—what kind of boots are you walking in—you see, I'm an expert. [*looks under the table*].

GENTLEMAN: Oh, I'm wearing quite well-made ones—you could hardly tell I've got one short leg.

HOLTFRETER: Yes, that's exactly what I thought right away, sir; how did you come by this leg?

GENTLEMAN: *laughs*] How? Quite naturally—I've had it since birth.

HOLTFRETER: No, you can't fool me! That leg was handed into me personally three days ago for repairs and then quite unexpectedly gave me the slip. That's the leg for which I accepted full responsibility and for that leg and its safe return, I've set the civic wheels in motion.

GENTLEMAN: *laughs*] Let it pass and have a glass of beer with me. [ELIAS *brings glasses*].

HOLTFRETER: Let it pass? No, no, sir, I'm personally responsible for that leg—do I have to call the police?

GENTLEMAN: I'll spare you the trouble; if I am suspected of appearing in a stolen leg then I'll accompany you to the police station with it. Does that make you happy? Cheers!

HOLTFRETER: But I shall really have to be on my toes, that leg has a devil of a fast step and is attached to a devil of a backside—cheers!

GENTLEMAN: Well, that's that settled for the time being—a devil of a backside, you say! [*raps himself on the thigh*] But apart from that, I mean, the rest of it, the skin and bones, etc., are all perfectly respectable—besides, you know—I am a lover of humanity.

HOLTFRETER: Of course, I didn't want to suggest you weren't.

GENTLEMAN: Incidentally, that's yet another example for you—growing and becoming work in curious ways.

HOLTFRETER: How do you mean?

GENTLEMAN: You can't spit without hitting some spot, where something is waiting to be created, waiting to get out of its cocoon. Look—what became of the leg today—am I not a reasonable fellow grown from a devil of a backside? Becoming: that is the password!

ELIAS: Am I right in thinking you are looking for the Prayer House, sir?

GENTLEMAN: Quite right, I have friends there, but I'm afraid I'm too late, and I'm in good company here too—I'm with friends everywhere, prayer house or pub, we and you are all on the same paths of becoming, on the move towards better things, even on Devil's legs.

ELIAS: A beautiful and edifying non with our beer, all for nothing.

GENTLEMAN: Your servant—for nothing. Beer has to be paid for, recognition is our only reward. Always onwards, always something new, always more into the open—that's how it is with us—as we were saying, all for nothing.

HOLTFRETER? My name is Holtfreter, sir.

GENTLEMAN: Well?

HOLTFRETER: That business about becoming must stop somewhere, for, sir, if it goes on and on like that and we go on developing towards infinite grandeur, then we won't know ourselves in the end.

GENTLEMAN: Is that bad? Do you want to be Holtfreter for ever—is it worth while? But it is worth while to become someone who is ashamed he ever was Holtfreter.

HOLTFRETER: Ashamed, sir?

GENTLEMAN: If you're not, you never will be—incidentally, do you know somebody called Mr. Virgin here, and can you take me to his house? We can look in at the police station on the way if you like. As we go, I'll tell you what I mean by being ashamed.

HOLTFRETER: For Heaven's sake, take your time with that devil of a leg—Mr. Virgin lives just off the market square on the right. [HOLTFRETER *and* GENTLEMAN *off*].

IST CUSTOMER: Come on Elias. I'm still thirsty.

ELIAS: No more tonight. Your thirst is still becoming and will become even grander, but your credit is still in its cocoon, so they don't tally.

2ND CUSTOMER: *to* 3RD] We all go the same way home. [*all three off.* GRETA *comes back*, BOLL *after her, and grabs her by the arm.* ELIAS *clears up*].

BOLL: It is an awful lot to ask, Greta—after all you're an intelligent woman and know that I am somebody who doesn't generally

waste time pleading. Alright, you shall have everything, do you
hear?

GRETA: How slim you are, Blue Boll—that's what you like to hear,
isn't it?

BOLL: Didn't I promise you everything, everything, Greta?

GRETA: How young, Blue Boll—do you like that?

BOLL: Do you imagine you have to torment me, you witch?

GRETA: Aren't you the one who knows no MUST, Blue Boll—do
you like that even more?

BOLL: If you say it, I have to like it. Yes, Greta, say it again.

GRETA: There is no MUST for you—even if you are Blue Boll!

BOLL: More, more.

GRETA: I love you, Blue Boll, does that please you?

BOLL: It does me good—more than I like to admit, more, more.

GRETA: Boll must—he has to take it, has to feel ashamed, has to
listen to a lot more besides.

BOLL: I'm listening, Greta, say it again if you feel like it.

GRETA: All for pleasure—evil pleasure, Blue Boll, are you listening?

BOLL: I hear.

GRETA: You shall have nothing from me, I give you nothing—even
if you do tell me again that you want to help me, Boll must, one
way or the other.

ELIAS: Oh you lot, what a life! Why don't you go to bed? But if you
haven't reached that stage yet, well wait for the good time, broach
a barrel of new time, don't save up any remnants of the old—
becoming is the password. [*he pushes over a chair for* GRETA *and
makes her sit down*].

BOLL: What kind of place is this—at dead of night and in the middle
of the street?

ELIAS: Oh, the police turn a blind eye—we get along fine—all sorts
of people are well looked after here—it's alright for you to sit
down.

BOLL: *sits down at the other side of the table*]What have you got to
offer here, then?

ELIAS: Finest possible selection, delicacies for the lordliest palates.
You just have to order.

BOLL: Have you ever heard of Maraschino?

ELIAS: My wife, sire, is sleeping the sleep of the just and it is her
constant and unchanging custom to sleep with the keys under her

pillow—can't get at the cabinet with the good things, unfortunately, unfortunately! But the crude everyday medicine chest is eager for you to make its acquaintance, sir.

BOLL: I can see what you're getting at, you can keep your poison.

ELIAS: *places himself right in front of him, legs wide apart*] As I said already—becoming, sir, is the password—there's no telling where we'll land up with all the grandeur. You too, sir, are singled out for great things. What I'm saying is, do you want to be Blue Boll for ever? Is it worth while? [*when he tries to get up, makes him stay*] You have a head for that and your becoming will rage rampant. In this vale of comfort you can safely graze.

BOLL: How do you know who I am? Basically I have very little to do with Blue Boll, practically nothing, in fact.

ELIAS: Practically nothing, nor I suppose has the little lady?

BOLL: That is her business—anyway I have nothing to do with her. And if I were Blue Boll would you like to change places with me?

ELIAS: Or you with me perhaps? Round these parts they call me Elias the Devil. [*whispering*] And I can tell you confidentially, between ourselves—there is something to it!

BOLL: In that case, let's forget the change-over, shall we—the devil, no less? In what way are you most aware of it, your devilishness, I mean—what are the symptoms? Don't you find that all things considered I really talk downright nicely to you?

ELIAS: Oh, I am thoroughly accustomed to speaking with men of honour—but it's wrong to over-estimate the advantages of that. Yes, Mr. Boll, as far as being a devil is concerned—you know, you just have to be one wholeheartedly, then it's alright. Every man is his own best neighbour, an honourable and respectable neighbour, of course—if you manage that more or less, then you make a nice little devil. And then—you mustn't get scared, least of all at yourself. Can the devil be afraid of devils? You lot who don't want to change places with any devil, you won't do it, because you're just a jumble of fears and don't know that the devil is something whole. You can't be what you want to be; you don't want to be what you have to be: half-people are no devils. [*sticks out his hand*] Grab hold and give me your half and I'll give you a shot of hell for it. As for me—what use would a miserable half like you be to me here? [*blows his nose into his hand and sticks it out again*] Like that—and it's gone!

BOLL: Oh, stop your bloody hocus-pocus—Devil take you!

ELIAS: And the little lady—she looks as if she'll have nothing to do with half-people.

BOLL: Bah—and anyway, why should I cast off Blue Boll? Every man is his own best neighbour.

ELIAS: Exactly, exactly—away with Blue Boll, in the end that would be the best thing for him. [laughs].

BOLL: What have you got to laugh at so stupidly?

ELIAS: I'm glad I'm not Blue Boll, I'm just Elias, the Devil, but something whole, thank God. What Elias does he has to do, and what Elias has to do, he wants to do—think of me what you will, and if you think I was eavesdropping on what the little lady was whispering, then you're right. There *was* somebody out there in the dark and I heard something like: Boll must, one way or the other.

BOLL: Is that how it came out?

ELIAS: *to* GRETA] Any different?

GRETA: Yes, that's how it came out and it's true.

ELIAS: *to* GRETA] As for you, my little coffin, something dead has crawled inside you—Elias is the man for you there, he'll put you on your feet again. My dear little lady, many's the one I've helped here, you're perfectly safe here. A lovely room and you are tired too—have a good sleep, have a bit of shut-eye, and be as silent as you want. No, you say? Do you know what you are refusing? Take note—see first, then say. See then say, that's the time to say no, if bed and room don't please you. You go in there and lock the door behind you and tomorrow is another day. [catches hold of her, though she resists and pushes her into the house] Gently, gently, don't wake up my old lady, go straight ahead, quietly. [to BOLL, who has leapt to his feet] Maybe you would like some of my poison after all? Too late, we're closing up and there is no lodging here for people as grand as Blue Boll. [closes the door after him, BOLL is left standing in the darkness].

BOLL: Away with Boll—and he is not even allowed to ask whether he wants to or has to? Haven't I got the bridle in my teeth? What's the use—I must wait till there's a pull on the reins to show me where to next.

VIRGIN, GENTLEMAN, HOLTFRETER, *the latter in humble attitude behind the* GENTLEMAN.

HOLTFRETER: The street gets very crooked here and the light from the market place gets rubbed thin on all the bends. Isn't that somebody standing there?

BOLL: No other.

VIRGIN: We are looking for Elias's Inn, round about here, can you help us?

BOLL: *knocks*] Elias, hey, Elias—customers!

ELIAS: *from an upper window*] Nothing doing, Mr. Boll. Customers can clear off pretty smartly.

VIRGIN: What's this I hear—Mr. Boll and standing there in the dark? [*to the* GENTLEMAN] The same Mr. Boll of whom you have very probably heard. You see, Mr. Boll, this gentleman is a stranger here and would like to spend the night—why it has to be here certainly looks extremely mysterious, but he's simply looking for a chance to change Elias's devilish outlook a bit. We of the Brotherhood are right next-door to Elias, and, oh, my God . . .

GENTLEMAN: I am delighted to meet you Mr. Boll. You probably don't think much of the prospect of accommodation at Elias's either?

BOLL: Go right ahead and start your parley with him anyway. Maybe Elias is human after all. [GENTLEMAN *talks with* ELIAS].

HOLTFRETER: *to* BOLL] Mr. Boll—oh, Mr. Boll—the things that happen—such things, Mr. Boll. This gentleman here, the unknown gentleman—who do you think he might be?

BOLL: Well, who could he be?

HOLTFRETER: To cut it short: the Lord God himself, as a simple pilgrim. Embracing us all in participation—in short, the Lord Himself. I was the first to recognize Him and I take some credit for it.

BOLL: Do you want me to be surprised? This kind of thing is in the air, it's full of it, the air brings it, the air delivers it up—if he's not somebody different altogether, then he must be God Himself.

VIRGIN: Have you any idea how worried I was about you, Mr. Boll?

BOLL: Too good of you, Mr. Virgin, I am very grateful for so much—eh, solicitude.

VIRGIN: You know, I was waiting hour after hour for the church tower key—waiting and thinking: oh, God, Mr. Boll is clambering around in the tower and maybe he'll fall.

BOLL: Accidentally.

172

VIRGIN: Accidentally—yes, accidentally.

BOLL: On purpose.

VIRGIN: No-one can know what's going to happen next—you were so unusual in speech and general behaviour this morning, Mr. Boll—what about the key now?

BOLL: Quite right, the key! But look, I don't know my way around my own pocket in the dark, wait till tomorrow. [*to himself*] One says—away with Boll; the other thinks he'll plunge like a thunderclap and hailstorm from the spire—I'm curious to see how Boll's becoming turns out.

GENTLEMAN: Well, we'll just have to resign ourselves to it—Elias is clearly not inclined to offer me hospitality. [*to* VIRGIN] Where to now?

BOLL: To the 'Golden Orb' with my Lord, to the 'Golden Orb'. I'm on my way there myself. You are my guest, Sire, even incognito—I am grateful for the opportunity of offering my services to help you out. May I count myself fortunate in having you accept?

GENTLEMAN: Yes, Mr. Boll, so that your kindness will not be wasted, I accept gladly.

BOLL: *to himself*] Greta has the Devil for a sleeping partner, I go home with God—it's enough to give one funny ideas.

5

Hotel lounge in the 'Golden Orb'. Otto Prunkhorst on the sofa behind a barricade of bottles. Mrs. Boll opposite him.

MRS. BOLL: Yes, Otto, if you put it that way, you see . . .

OTTO: Absolutely, and . . . to sum it up . . . absolutely.

MRS. BOLL: I just want to ask: what are we women supposed to do if the men have the nerve to do this kind of thing—and then you suggest they do it without guile and in all innocence.

OTTO: In all innocence, quite right, you see, it's true. Men are always more innocent than women—incidentally, are we talking about any men in particular?

MRS. BOLL: But, Otto, how you keep flirting with forgetfulness, do you still know what you are saying after all that wine?

OTTO: As long as I can still order audibly, I keep drinking. Look, how do you think we sit it out in our place at Goldensee, Martha? Bertha goes to bed early, as she always does and always has done since before we were married—so—what can I do, how can I get round it, I have to do all the sitting up late by myself, and get through the claret on my own. And today I have to take on the responsibility for drinking Kurt's share—haven't I, Martha?

MRS. BOLL: Well, we'll just have to wait for him, for even if he has sent a message that we are not to wait, he doesn't really mean it, does he?

OTTO: Dead right, quite agree, Martha. [*bangs on the table*] Let him think I'd creep off to bed before him if he wants to, as if I needed his permission to nip off. Here I sit and here I sup until the matter has been fully looked into and that will be very soon at the very latest! And then, I'm funny that way, but the more I drink, the quicker I finish off the bottles, and the smoother my thoughts flow.

MRS. BOLL: Listen, Otto. Do you believe that people can change, I mean so much that they become absolutely different people? You must appreciate I am more afraid for Kurt than I like to say.

OTTO: *laughs*] If Kurt is that way inclined, then he will have to do it off his own bat. If he insists on annoying us with it too, then I'll show him a thing or two. We don't want him any different from what he is—absolutely no change!

MRS. BOLL: Yes, but . . .

OTTO: *bangs on the table*] I am against any change. Things can't become any better and therefore we're better off without any becoming whatsoever—that's all there is to it! Rest assured, Martha, I'll explain it to him harshly enough—Bertha's another— she's against any change and that's why she has gone to bed at her regular hour, and that is what's so marvellous about Bertha, Martha, you must see that— —Pipelow!

Waiter comes, OTTO *points to the empty bottle,* PIPELOW *fetches a fresh one.*

MRS. BOLL: You know, Otto, Kurt often lets himself be got at unawares—yes, he says then, what ought to be is that it oughtn't to be—or something like that, so . . .

OTTO: Quite right, Martha, that's why it's alright for him to kick over the traces occasionally. I just can't see why he has to seek my presence, so that he can be conspicuous by his absence.

MRS. BOLL: *quietly*] I believe he is somebody, we just don't know what kind of somebody. That's why he maybe can't help it if we are puzzled by him. In the end he's maybe more puzzled by us than we are by him.

BOLL, GENTLEMAN *and* HOLTFRETER.

BOLL: How time flies, who would have thought it—as late as that already! Well, I hope you haven't deprived yourselves of anything. Well under way, Otto? Evening, Martha.

OTTO: You might well ask how we've been managing! What I want to know is what's the point of arranging to meet if firstly you don't come and secondly my wife goes—do you think secondly Bertha likes waiting?

BOLL: Didn't I phone several times, didn't they give you any message that I was still held up?

OTTO: Oh, sure, and the rest. Just a phone call, is that all?

MRS. BOLL: Couldn't you have had me called to the phone, Kurt?

BOLL: Why? Out of pure consideration, Martha, what was the point in disturbing you while you ate? Eat, I thought, let her eat in peace, people who are eating have their mouths full and chew into the telephone—no, I thought, leave her in peace—by the way, Otto, take note, Martha, what will you say to this, I must introduce you. This gentleman is my guest, his name is undisclosed and secret, but don't be startled, my children: he is our Lord God Himself, strictly incognito, of course, privately, as it were—and here to act as guarantor and corroborator of my words, also without name so far . . .

HOLTFRETER: Holtfreter is my name, Master Shoemaker. [*bows humbly to* GENTLEMAN] With His permission.

GENTLEMAN: *to* BOLL] If you don't mind, Mr. Boll, I won't lift the cloak of anonymity in which you have clothed me—only just a little and on occasion, confidentially between us two: yes, Mr. Boll—Lord God you say—well, between ourselves there is something to it. I accept the name Lord, in the sense that I may be a weak and humble reflection out of eternity, a faint, scarcely perceptible shadow of God. That's what you meant, wasn't it?

BOLL: No unnecessary humility, sir. I know how to show proper respect for my guests—so Otto, keep your seat at the back, the Lord God will sit beside you, the two of you together will produce a majestic symmetry. Now then, Martha, stay in your chair, have you sampled all the finest numbers? [*they arrange themselves as indicated*].

OTTO: I always pictured God quite differently—personally, I have never asked him what his profession was, but you can imagine for yourselves, what I think. I am a land-owner, you are a land-owner, that is quite sufficient for to-day and for longer, what do we need the Lord God's company for? Yes, you know, Kurt, every man is his own best neighbour, my wife has gone to bed, you see.

BOLL: What lovely white teeth Bertha still has, Otto, but they are now with her in bed. God preserve her teeth for many a year yet, I should have very much liked our dear Lord God to admire her in them this evening, but as you rightly say, every man is his own best neighbour—she got tired and—by the way, tell me, but no, I don't want to upset you and her with any more tonight.

OTTO: If you really mean it, Kurt, I could ask her a minute. Naturally her teeth, her teeth, there's absolutely nothing you can say against her teeth, you're right.

BOLL: Fill up the glasses, Otto. [OTTO *pours*] You know—but don't take offence at this—when I see you in operation, Otto—there's a fearful family resemblance! I am afraid we resemble each other fearfully—it has often occurred to me how crushing the phenomenon of family resemblance like this is—floors you, you know—but don't take offence, d'you hear! Now your wife's teeth, how long do you think she'll have them—and anyway, does she want to stay Bertha Prunkhorst for ever—is it worth while?

HOLTFRETER: *gets up and with respectful humility to the* GENTLEMAN] With His permission! [*to* BOLL] That's it, Mr. Boll, that's it exactly. It is not worth while, nay more, on the contrary, it is worth while to get to the point where one is ashamed ever to have been such a lady. You are so right, Mr. Boll. [*sits*].

BOLL: I had not appealed to you directly, Mr. Holtfreter, that is your name isn't it, and you are obviously a shoemaker—good. Strictly speaking, you do not know the lady in question.

HOLTFRETER: *get up and with respectful humility to the* GENTLEMAN] With His permission! All of us sitting here together will feel ashamed one day, and the lady too, thank God. [*sits down, then more quietly*] Because it does not matter whether I know the lady, if I only know in what respect she can feel ashamed, that is, in respect to the 'becoming splendour'. In this respect all ladies are alike.

OTTO: All the same, Kurt, are we going to go on like this, or how do you see it, Kurt? [*to* HOLTFRETER] You are going to knock over the bottles if you keep jumping up and down like that. Kurt, next time you come to Goldensee, you must be sure to have a look at Antonia—she's a pure Jersey, you know—fabulous milkers—and, yes—what else, what was the other thing I wanted to say?

GENTLEMAN: *takes his glass*] You've a remarkably steady hand, sir, I noticed that immediately. If you permit me: your health, and, of course, above all, that of the ladies, present and absent. [*they clink glasses*].

OTTO: Steady, steady, oh, a very steady hand, and besides, another thing—don't you know the other thing I wanted to say [*to* MRS. BOLL] God, Martha, we were talking about it all evening, what was it again?

MRS. BOLL: On no account, Otto, do me just this one favour and let it pass for this evening.

OTTO: Yes, that's it, a favour or something like that—no, not a favour, but it was something to do with somebody favouring some woman. [*to* BOLL] What was all this about some woman, Kurt, you know, some woman or other and then you are supposed to have assumed responsibility for some woman, maybe the same woman, Kurt, eh, assumed it absolutely—[*triumphantly to* MRS BOLL]—There you are, Martha, did you think I'd forget something we'd gone into so fully?

MRS. BOLL *covers her eyes.*

HOLTFRETER: *gets up and with respectful humility to the* GENTLEMAN] With His permission! That woman, that same woman, is Greta, and I am her uncle. [*to* BOLL] The oath Mr. Boll took is as good as a civic ceremony. As good as Mr. Boll is good. They call my Greta the witch of Parum, but that has nothing to do with the responsibility that Mr. Boll has had placed between his teeth, and my brother-in-law Grüntal, the husband of that same woman, has gone back quite happily to Parum to his three children, the very ones who are also Greta's three children. [*sits down*].

OTTO: Three's not nearly enough children to make it worth your while telling me about them. But look here, Kurt, tell me: what about this woman and this shoemaker uncle—is she a witch, a real witch? [*gets up*].

BOLL: Yes, yes, what more do you want, isn't that enough? I should have thought that was more than enough—do sit down Otto!

OTTO: A real witch, Kurt?

BOLL: And I have found her a room with a real devil, what's more. [*to* GENTLEMAN] Sir, you mustn't try to look for any evil intention in the fact that we keep discussing this brood in your presence. [*to* OTTO] Do sit down, Otto!

GENTLEMAN: I too am friendly with devils and witches, we are all on the same path.

OTTO: Kurt, I will not sit down, I had to promise Martha I wouldn't, I had to give her my hand on it. I mayn't sit down as long as I am a decent fellow. And that remark about fearful family resemblance, that's alright—I can just as easily apply it to you. I feel ashamed, Kurt, thank God, it's a frightening realization, I feel ashamed of the family resemblance—Martha, poor Martha! [*gives her his hand; she sobs*].

MRS. BOLL: Sit down, Otto, it is much too late to think of getting anything like enough sleep now. Shouldn't I order coffee?

OTTO: Do that, Martha, coffee does you good, so it's a good idea. But sit—no, that I cannot do. [MRS. BOLL, *in tears off*] There you are, Kurt, see what you've accomplished. I am ashamed that I ever had to promise Martha anything of the sort. Why can't we discuss all this quietly between ourselves?

BOLL: If you did promise her, Otto, I am sure the intention was never that this should be talked over quietly, but that all the usual family pressures etc. would be brought to bear.

HOLTFRETER: *gets up and with respectful humility to the* GENTLEMAN] With His permission! I take some pride in drawing your attention to the fact that from this morning on, becoming has been proceeding gloriously in our city. And even at an hour so late that coffee has to be made, becoming in its eternally effortless vigour has clearly gained fresh impetus. And humbly and not without taking some pride in it, I draw the attention of all and sundry to the presence of the—[*bows to the* GENTLEMAN]—as prime mover. [*sits down*].

MRS. BOLL *comes back.*

OTTO: Ah, Martha, thank God, Martha, we badly need Pipelow,

because he will fix the coffee, or has he too gone to bed already?

MRS. BOLL: I couldn't just walk right past her door, so I looked in to see Bertha, Otto—Bertha absolutely forbids any coffee drinking whatsoever, and you are to come to bed immediately, Otto! [*to* BOLL] Saugwurm's getting the coach ready—we've never left so late.

OTTO: What? No coffee? My dear Martha, did you have to go and tell Bertha of all people about the coffee? That was inexcusably attentive of you, I feel. [*to* GENTLEMAN] If you wanted to get up I would gladly let you past—did you say something to that effect?

GENTLEMAN: Before I trouble you, sir, I should like to ask you something.

OTTO: Before you ask, be kind enough to consider that I absolutely never lend money except on principle.

GENTLEMAN: There'll be no mention of money. I should even be in the fortunate position of being able to help *you* out with a small sum in the event of need.

OTTO: In the event of need? Do you think I, or any of us, need money? I am not aware that I frequent any such circles, you seem to know such people—our circles are never in need.

GENTLEMAN: Unfortunately there are many good and needy people among my friends. Meanwhile if not in need of this kind, we are all joined together in need, in the other sense, aren't we?

OTTO: This is becoming more preposterous every minute. In the other sense—you can't mean me with you in the other whatsit? Or am I drunk?

GENTLEMAN: Neither in that regrettable state nor in a state of sobriety will it escape you that your earlier phrase about the fearful resemblance expressly indicates the need for some transformation in your family, that is to say, presumably some amelioration. Or to express it more simply, you feel that your present condition absolutely demands a change for the better.

OTTO: You know, Kurt, why don't we just send these people away, eh? I think this Lord God fellow has drunk enough wine he's not paying for.

BOLL: What do you mean, send him away, he is living in the 'Golden Orb' like yourself and he's my guest. [*slaps him on the shoulder*] My God, Otto, your words come from the knots and gnarls of the fibre of your being. Good God, us in need! I'd like to know what we'd be doing there, what would we ever be in need of, I'd just like to have somebody show us what. Are we in need of transformation—trans-for-ma-tion?

OTTO: Eh, old fellow?

BOLL: *to* GENTLEMAN] In that case it cannot have escaped you that my cousin is not guilty of coining the wicked phrase about family resemblance?

GENTLEMAN: Your cousin picked it up certainly—but it's a good phrase, not a wicked one, Mr. Boll! There's the seed of something in it—readiness stirring, the first shoots of becoming. [*to* OTTO] Great changes await you too, very soon, not only you, Mr. Prunkhorst, we all share in the joy of what's happening, we all stand fused and joined together in the sad state of the general and fearful family resemblance of the human condition, don't we?

OTTO: I'm drunk, but not so drunk that I couldn't see clean through his ridiculous divinity—he's an impostor, Kurt, an impostor, I tell you!

GENTLEMAN: Exactly, Mr. Prunkhorst, an impostor, a witch, a devil, on the same path as you and everybody else. Consider the fine behaviour of Mr. Boll: he accepts responsibility for the witch, in him too the first shoots of becoming are piercing the crust, and you mustn't feel hurt, sir—we are all in this deeper sense associates and brothers of witches and devils—yourself included!

OTTO: *swings his fists*] Kurt, I appeal to you, get a hold of yourself— hubuh—why is the flag of my hurt feelings waving about? Why is it reeling? Now Kurt, I appeal to you—renounce—the state of all change. Stand fast, old fellow, in the state of matrimony and stand fast in the state before matrimony and behind matrimony and beside matrimony, and collar whom you will, witches for all I care, and above all stand fast in the state of no-responsibility, stand fast in that! Renounce responsibility! [SAUGWURM *appears at the door. Half-choking to him*] Saugwurm! This is a bit of luck, here comes Saugwurm spooking along, old Saugwurm, there is a spitoon in the corner on your left, see it? Yes, that's it, pass it over, will you? [*places the spitoon in front of the* GENTLEMAN, *pours in dregs out of bottles*] Now, you fortune-teller, you hangman's apprentice, you spelling mistake on a lavatory wall, you pre-digested dinner, you much-used convenience, you lost cause, I advise you to beware of my steady hand, and see if you can enjoy what my sense of responsibility spews out for you. [*to* BOLL] Do you renounce responsibility?

BOLL *signs to* SAUGWURM *to take the spitoon away again.* OTTO *tries to speak, stops and sits down again.*

SAUGWURM: The coach is ready when you are. [*off*].

MRS. BOLL: Thank Heavens we can be off at last.

BOLL: Be off—home? Me? No, Greta, we'll not be off!

MRS. BOLL: Greta, you say?

BOLL: No, not now or any other time, Greta. If I did go, I would head straight for hell. Greta in the clutches of the devil—and you expect me to drive off? Greta, who knows not what she does, Greta, whose guardian I am, who wants to set fire to the tents where dwell the souls of her children, and Greta, whom I have promised to assist in this, instead of helping her to accomplish the opposite!

MRS. BOLL: Don't listen to him. For my part I'll save up my forgiveness for later, and he shall have it. But now he *must*—he must leave with us!

OTTO: *with difficulty*] I'd better haul my flag down to half-mast—anything else I can do to help, poor Martha; shall I appeal to him once more? [*tries to muster enough strength*].

MRS. BOLL: Oh, Otto, what would be the use—I can hardly understand our dear Lord any more, for what could He possibly intend with us since His intentions are clearly quite different from ours—no, oh, no!

BOLL: So, dear Martha, you are prepared to forgive me? But just tell me this: What use is your forgiveness to me if I don't forgive myself? There, there, there is my case of need, the case of cases. Can't you imagine the following: outside the silent night and me, Boll himself, in the tower struggling up the steps, and what does the tower say to it? It says Boll must! And then the silent night breathes a tiny breath of air, just one and quite secretly—from above and unseen, but a heavy, heavy fragment of night comes crashing down with this breath of air and smashes the pavement in two and in the morning they scrub half a dozen yards of Boll's blood off the stones. Just imagine all the unnecessary fuss and please realize once and for all—rather than hurtle off with Saugwurm and your dear hand in mine to hell I'll hurtle through the air and turn somersaults on the way down.

MRS. BOLL: It's just—just—it's just an attempt to scare me, or what else do you expect me to do?

BOLL: Don't you understand? Listen carefully, because this morning I just stood there, when you were the suffering woman, hurt pride and silence—you know—so now you are to be honoured before all the people, for all the people must recognize that yours is the great honour of decision. Between you, you and the tower, you share equal power over me, you both speak and advise, and you both decide. Rise up in triumph, Martha, you are called.

MRS. BOLL: Oh God, I feel so terribly afraid, what are you thinking of, Kurt, how am I supposed to understand all this straight off? [BOLL *raises a finger and wags it as if he wished to listen without disturbance. All look at him,* MRS. BOLL *scans the faces of the others for some explanation, looking finally at the* GENTLEMAN *who smiles to her*].

GENTLEMAN: *quietly*] Must Boll?

MRS. BOLL: *with short sob to* BOLL] You must, Kurt, you must go to her, I send you to her, go to Greta, Kurt, go now!

6

Bedroom in the 'Devil's Kitchen Inn', a door in the back wall, bed and table right, where there is also just room for a window on to the yard of the house, left an old arm-chair, on the table a kitchen lamp giving little light. Greta is sitting on the bed dressed, and seems to be listening to some noises, suddenly she puts her hands over her ears. On the other side of the window-pane a fist appears, it knocks. Greta jumps, looks about her, goes to the window and opens it. Elias's head shoots up into the light.

ELIAS: *whispering*] Take and eat and drink—I'll be back soon and meanwhile you can—come on, grab hold, what I've scraped together for you isn't at all bad.

GRETA: I don't want to—you know what I want—nothing to eat, nothing to drink, no presents.

ELIAS: This is no present—eating and drinking is all part of it, you know? Eat and drink, then you'll be the way I want you. Your hollow-eyed look certainly means hunger, you have to be gay if you please, being gay is part of it—agreed? [*she takes the parcel*] Now, you see, you're a good girl and we'll get on alright and not grudge each other anything. Listen, I have to come in from the yard, my wife sleeps next the passage and there are so many loose boards—I've got some more work to do—that's business. [*off*].

GRETA *lays the package on the table. There is a knock on the wall.* GRETA *listens, shakes her head, more knocking.*

GRETA: *quietly*] I'm here.

WEHDIG'S VOICE: *behind the left wall*] Aren't you Greta?

GRETA: I'm here.

VOICE: I'm so hungry and hear talk of food and drink: how's a man to sleep if there's talk of food and drink next door?

GRETA: You can eat, come and get it.

Sound of a bed creaking; then scraping and groping in the dark, and through the centre door from the corridor comes WEHDIG *half-dressed and in bare feet.*

WEHDIG: Well?

GRETA *points to the table.*

WEHDIG: Good appetite, Monsieur Wehdig! [*unwraps the package, shakes a bottle*] Glug, glug; from the sound it's not something for washing with, lovely, clear golden colour, I'll keep it for later. [*chews*] Where is he anyway—gone? You two got any plans; if not I'll just stay here—eh?

GRETA: Where do all the people come from?

WEHDIG: What people?

GRETA: The ones you can hear.

WEHDIG: *stops chewing, listens, shakes his head*] No—plenty of lice tramping around, but no people. [*chews and stares at* GRETA].

GRETA: He is moving among them, saying something. Elias is saying something.

WEHDIG: Well, what is he saying, then?

GRETA: He's raging at them.

WEHDIG: That all? If he is cursing that will keep him occupied—all the better if he's cursing.

GRETA: I suppose he's angry.

WEHDIG: Yes, angry—blow out the light, otherwise he'll think of something to do in here too with us. [*he blows out the light himself*].

GRETA: There's still light there too—shining through. [*points to the left wall*].

WEHDIG: Behind that wall is the hole he put me in. [*laughs*] He forgot to take the shift off me—oh well, doesn't matter to you, with or without it's all the same, eh?

GRETA: Still more people!

WEHDIG: The more the merrier; forget it.

GRETA: But what can they be doing, is there room for so many?

WEHDIG: Do they worry about me? I don't worry about them.

GRETA: *goes to the wall*] You can see through the cracks—oh, Elias is there too, running about, bringing dishes and things, and slaving away, pretty hard.

WEHDIG: Why don't you come over here; you can sit on my knee if you like, Greta.

GRETA: Oh, good Heavens!

WEHDIG: Well, what do you want—that's my little room through that wall, I told you—that's all, no people, no Elias—come on, Greta, you're imagining things.

GRETA: Aren't they playing with golden playing cards? I do believe that they have gold cards in their hands—they tinkle when they fall, they really are cards of pure gold.

WEHDIG: Say what you like, I'll soon be finished eating, then you'll see.

GRETA: Yes, they are gambling with gold cards and Elias—just look, Elias is grabbing them by their legs and tearing their boots off. And now—he's dragging up tubs, steaming hot, and pushing them under the table and two by two he makes them stick their feet into the tubs. I am sure these tubs are red hot! Look, look, look—there he comes with a cauldron full of hot coals and the other fellow at the top, I know him, that's Mehlspeis, Mehlspeis with his raven's beak, Mehlspeis is forced in—ooh, ooh, ooh, how it scorches him, he's sweating clear fat like bacon in the frying pan and the hot drops are jumping like fleas—Mehlspeis holds gold cards in his hand too and plays them—but his face as he plays, I shouldn't like to play that game with gold cards!

WEHDIG: Yes, the lovely sizzling noise of bacon in the pan always makes you prick up your ears—can you smell it too, Greta?

GRETA: Oh, God, the horrible faces they're all making, trying to look as though they're enjoying it as you're supposed to when you're gambling, shuffling their gold cards and playing on. Yes, yes, you lot, you have to put some kind of face on it, however hard it may be. But I must say this, you are doing your best, you don't want anybody to call you spoil-sports.

WEHDIG: My feet are cold, I can hold out longer than they can.

GRETA: Here comes old Splint too and behind him somebody else I know, Käselow from Klüz and Grundbarsch too, yes, that's who it is—but he is dead long since and Splint too, and I saw Käselow buried myself; how did they get here?

WEHDIG: Oh well, Greta, you'd better ask them; they'll probably remember how they got here.

GRETA: We always used to call Käselow, Bramble Georgie—he's still got his red growths dangling from his cheeks—oh, oh, Elias is starting to make a row, somebody not being let in? He's coming in anyway, pushes Elias aside, and why! I know him too, that must be Boll, but Boll when young, slim and ruddy, and he is lighting his cigar and blowing the smoke down Elias's throat. I wonder what he has there, why is he hunting in his pocket—pulling out a little ball of gold and making it jump on the palm of his hand. His head is turning right round backwards over his shoulders, I am scared he is looking for me.

WEHDIG: *gets up*] Now then, Greta, the sociable part of the evening is about to commence. Let's examine what's swimming around in the bottle—you must have a spot too, Greta.

GRETA: *groans*] Oh, no, are you there as well, all three of you? Oh, you poor little creatures, what do you want in hell? Your feet are so dirty from walking so far, and your worst clothes on—how lost you look standing there and nobody pays any attention to you! It's a good thing your head can turn round backwards, Blue Boll, because you see them and wave with your long cigar—and Elias leaves Boll alone, understands and laughs at them and drags out tiny little chairs; sit down and rest your tired feet—now he's pulling off their dirty boots, first Ali's, then Lina's then Petie's, pulling off their boots and waving his arms, and now he's seizing hold of a cauldron with hot coals. [*screams*] Hey, Elias, what are you doing, they're my children, Elias, Elias, Elias; curse you, Elias!

WEHDIG: Woman, will you be quiet! This is the middle of the night, you'll rouse the whole house!

GRETA: *louder*] Mercy, Elias, or I'll stick you in head first—have mercy on my children, they are looking for me with their poor souls, you have nothing to do with them! [*she presses and beats against the wall*].

WEHDIG: That wasn't the arrangement at all, include me out, I wipe my mouth of this. [*he tries to put the bottle into his pocket, but it slips and rolls away and he fails to grab it*] Hope you poison whoever finds you. [*he slips away, the door remains open—*ELIAS *with light*].

ELIAS: Do you want to wear your tongue out, do you want to scream your throat to pieces? Till you choke, you witch!

GRETA: Who gave you permission to start on my children, you devil, Elias! [*she presses past him through the door, he holds her fast and presses her on to the bed, puts the light on the table*].

ELIAS: Children—yours—are you bewitched? [ELIAS' *wife* DORIS, *a massive woman with a bass voice and imperturbable manner, appears in the doorway*].

DORIS: She keeps having visitors, get rid of her, Elias—but make her pay first.

ELIAS: Go to bed, wife, everything will be taken care of. [DORIS *turns slowly and disappears*].

GRETA: Don't you know, all three are my children.

ELIAS: I know about the children, you told me earlier. [*quietly*] Be sensible, Greta, do you hear? Speak softly, the children—where are your children?

GRETA: In there—there where they're playing with gold cards and have their feet in the tubs, behind that wall—fetch them in here right away, Elias.

ELIAS: Have you eaten?

GRETA: He ate for me—he's in there with the others and Boll is there too playing with the little gold ball.

ELIAS: Oh, I see—yes, these locusts have always got their gut open, ready to shovel in whatever's going.

GRETA: Bring them, Elias, I beg you, bring all three of them.

ELIAS: Right away—quite right, it's as you say, Boll is in there feeding them. Boll is sure to find something for them.

GRETA: Let me go, Elias. Believe me, I am not afraid of these people, not even of Käselow and the other dead ones—I want to feed them myself, Elias.

ELIAS: Take it easy—look how out of breath you are.

GRETA: Listen, Elias, where do you keep your poison, could Boll not make a mistake and give them some of your poison?

ELIAS: Boll will do as he pleases, now this way, now that. Boll must, Greta—[DORIS *in the door*].

DORIS: Elias?

ELIAS: She is drunk, I'll have to tie her down. Go to bed. I'll have it all fixed in a sec. [DORIS *slowly off*].

GRETA: She isn't going in to them too, is she? She is a terrible woman, Elias, she mustn't go near the children.

ELIAS: Never eaten a child yet, and she isn't going in to them, Greta. She has children of her own.

GRETA: Children of her own—oh, Elias, what kind of children can they be!

ELIAS: Real children, healthy children, children the same as any other children, Greta.

GRETA: Real good children?

ELIAS: Couldn't be better.

GRETA: But where do you keep your poison, Elias, children will steal and are always searching for sweet things—what if they find the poison?

ELIAS: Well, what if they do, they've always been used to it, it doesn't do them any harm, they're so healthy, you can almost see them growing.

GRETA: What children they must be, what people you are!

ELIAS: That's how it is in business, happy in hell—now, Greta, you're beginning to see that everything is in order here, so I want to tell you something, but I'll tell you quietly—so that we won't forget the main thing— . . . [DORIS *at the door*].

DORIS: Elias?

ELIAS: Go to bed, wife.

DORIS: Elias.

ELIAS: You're to go to bed.

DORIS: Are you finished with her?

ELIAS: Go to bed, soon be ready.

DORIS: I think she's ready enough, go and call the police. I'll keep an eye on her. [*comes in*].

GRETA: Boll, Blue Boll, help!

DORIS: Is she—that one? Who would ever imagine she would do such things? Never mind the police. [*catches sight of the bottle, picks it up and puts it on the table. To* GRETA] You ought to be curry-combed to make you come to your senses. [*to* ELIAS] Didn't she say something about children?

ELIAS: What does it matter to you—children, what have her children got to do with us?

DORIS: It's got a lot to do with her children, we're quite prepared to lose some sleep over her children. [*sits down in the armchair*].

GRETA: Tell her, Elias, she mustn't, don't let her sit there.

ELIAS: You can say all that to her yourself, Greta, she is easy to get on with—a woman like her.

GRETA: I hear her drawing breath, Elias, I feel it as close as if the whole room were full of her, and she is just sitting there at the back. No, Elias, don't leave me.

ELIAS: You can say anything you like Greta, try it, you'll see. [*he busies himself, moves chairs, lifts up paper, turns the wick, every inch a hotel-keeper, only from time to time there is a grimace*].

DORIS: Everything will come to pass in its own good time, silly thing. You're tough, but I'll still eat you. [*wags her index-finger*] That is the devil, you silly thing—get thee behind him and come into my lap.

GRETA: *catches hold of* ELIAS] Do you hear, Elias, onto her lap, she says.

ELIAS: Do what you like, it all comes out the same in the end. [*to* DORIS] Can't you see she is afraid, wife? It's time you left her in peace.

DORIS: Oh, my Elias, how well I know you. She is afraid, but let her be, fear will help her, don't worry that fear might harm her. You learn that in this place.

GRETA: Oh, Elias, I know what she means, you learn with hot coals on your feet—weren't you on the point of putting the children's feet in the cauldron? What were they supposed to learn from hot coals?

DORIS: Come, my Elias, let's forget about the children, give me the bottle, just the thing for somebody like her—your poison, let me see, we'll see. [ELIAS *hands over the bottle*, DORIS *drinks*].

GRETA: In there? Is that it? Standing there on the table for all to see and you didn't say a thing about it?

DORIS: You know, my Elias, you can tell how good your intentions were with her from the taste of this bottle. Oho, you silly thing, so it takes someone who looks like you to win the warmth of his favour. Here, give her a drink, it'll drive the fear out of her, learn from the devils, learn how to put it away, learn how to get rid of such things.

GRETA: Don't you see, Elias, she is drinking and I have to after her?

ELIAS: Don't ask, do what she says, and don't act stupid—whatever I give you, that's what it's got to be. Oh, you are willing after all? Just look at her—she's drinking poison like water!

GRETA: *drinking*] Is this just the same as the hot coals? Oh, you poor children, your mother is to be consumed with internal fires.

DORIS: *wags her finger*] You silly thing, nobody gets burned by our coals. They know what they're doing, it's all very carefully done, it burns where it's needed, they only spoil what's spoiled already.

GRETA *doubles up*.

ELIAS: That's only the scalding shivers, Greta—it creeps into you and hardens your bowels and scorches out your fear, open your mouth wide, Greta.

DORIS: She's drinking alright, Elias, don't torment her.

GRETA: *drinking*] Ah, there's a lot to be learned from you people; it certainly burns, but it burns away the fear that was in the body and you don't need to worry about pain. [*looks towards the door*] I suppose they've come for their share too, eh, Elias?

THREE DEAD MEN *walk in*.

GRETA: That would suit you down to the ground, you bunch of creeps—eh, Käselow and Splint and Mehlspeis? You're the boys! [*laughs*] What have you done with your flesh and bone? I can't imagine how you are going to wish me 'Good morning'. Oh no, shaking hands with something that's been and gone, discarded, gone to earth, is not what my hand is for.

THE THREE DEAD MEN *look about them*.

GRETA: *laughs*] There's no mirror here, Mehlspeis. Oh, you, yes, it's alright for you to be proud—look at Splint, he's only half the man you are. Well, go on, laugh, you still have a bit of throat left.

MEHLSPEIS: Well, Greta, you know we're taking your children away with us, right now.

GRETA: Is that what you came for?

SPLINT. Yes. That's it exactly.

GRETA: The three of you?

KÄSELOW: We have to move off again right away, with the children.

GRETA: For you to keep—and then they have to turn into apparitions too in your fine company—and you must be starving too, you lot, you've lost a lot of flesh and your hollow-eyed look certainly means hunger. So you are lurking in wait for my children, are you? Have a drink first, nice drop of poison, it can't do you any harm, it will give you something else to think about. [*gives them a drink*].

SPLINT: As long as the children get their share, I don't mind if I do, I have room. [*drinks*].

GRETA: That must be a funny damned life when you're dead—but you must know best.

MEHLSPEIS: Yes, Greta, one gets by if one is not unreasonable—we'll look after the children. [*drinks*].

KÄSELOW: You can be easy in your mind, Greta, you soon get the hang of it and the young ones learn as quickly as the old. Once you start losing quick flesh you quickly put on foul flesh. [*drinks*].

GRETA: *laughs*] Swallow as much as you can, Käselow, now you can see you have scoffed the last drop and there's not a crumb, not a drop left—nothing, nothing, nothing left for Ali, nothing for Lina, nothing for Petie! Get going, you lot, on your way, all you're good for in your condition is to be good and dead. [THE THREE *look at each other*].

MEHLSPEIS: If only it wasn't all arranged, Greta.

GRETA: Just get the idea that it's all arranged out of your head—I didn't call you.

SPLINT: You can believe me, Greta, I am glad to do it. But I'd just as soon not. Greta, leave your brood of kids in the flesh, if you don't want them better off.

KÄSELOW: Should we bother to ask why? People like us have our pride and you'll have a long wait before an opportunity like this comes round again—I can't help you.

THE DEAD MEN *go off backwards.* GRETA *follows them and closes the door behind them.*

GRETA: Well, I managed that pretty well, didn't I? Do you think the dead all get so stupid when their reason rots? Didn't they look awful, they hardly had the sense to get back out thr ough the door. [*stands in front of* DORIS *and claps her hands*] And the poison is all drunk, all gone, nothing for Ali and Lina and Petie, not a drop, nothing left but an empty bottle!

DORIS *reaches out her arms,* GRETA *sinks down and hides herself in her lap.* ELIAS *has lain on the bed and is soon snoring.*

DORIS: Close, close, snuggle up warm, we'll forget which of us is which, forget everything including yourself, let yourself lie in a state of rest where all good things come from—give up all your sins and dreadful secrets, it does not bother me; what you confide to Elias' devil of a wife is buried in a safe place where it can do no harm, it will be overgrown and become part of me, and I can bear it and I bear it easily. Rest assured, you will become as free and unburdened as I become burdened. Let's have your block head here and I'll whisper in your ear.

GRETA: *gives her an ear*] Boll is—Boll is dead, Blue Boll is dead?

DORIS: Listen carefully. [*speaks softly*].

GRETA: Yes, that is true, I know. Blue Boll is sitting with his feet in Elias' hot cauldron—ow, ow, ow, Blue Boll, it goes boiling right up to your heart, there the bubbles burst, there the bad bunch blows on it with puffed-up cheeks—that's how it is, Blue Boll, that's how it has to be, she says. But what about young Boll, eh? Slim young Boll, who gives the children the little golden ball to play with, does he have to go into the hot coals?

DORIS: Doesn't have to, what he saves will be marked up to the credit of the Blue Boll—do you hear? [*speaks into her ear*].

GRETA: Is it no good, is it really no good, can he not forgive himself, can nobody do it, not even he? Oh, you poor Boll, I forgive you—play with the children and accept my forgiveness.

DORIS: That's the young one, you know, who is playing with the children.

GRETA: Yes, that's the young one; he does not have to atone for the crimes of the Blue. But if Doris can do so much, eat me up and suck me empty of evil, so that I become as free and unburdened of evil as she is full of it, can't she also exterminate Blue Boll, so that she bears him in herself too and still thrives?

DORIS: Let Blue Boll judge himself, you just be content—you have fallen into the hands of the devils who live in the house of evil, there much evil can find shelter. Elias snores and I too am weary—have accomplished something and shall build on it all in good time.

ELIAS: *in his sleep*] Boll must, this way or that. [*violent knocking is heard at the house door*].

GRETA: Is there still somebody trying to come in at this hour?

DORIS *sleeps and shaking has no effect*.

ELIAS: *in his sleep*] Boll must . . .

GRETA: That is Boll! [*she leaps up*] Boll, Blue Boll, wait, I'm coming! [*off*].

7

*Interior of the church, only one pillar, Gothic windows and pews visible.
A wooden apostle on the pillar. Greta is asleep on the pew. Boll is
walking up and down the aisle. The morning sun is shining through the
window and lighting up the apostle. A few minutes later Greta wakes
and sits up slowly, she follows Boll with her eyes, as he continues up and
down. As he comes past her they look at each other.*

GRETA: Isn't that Blue Boll—who else, but how did he get here?

BOLL: And you, Greta, aren't you here too? [*makes a gesture*] What a
house, Greta, what rockets of stone go soaring up and how
merrily everything leaps around up there in the arching heavens—
it's morning, Greta, have you slept well?

GRETA: Did Boll not give them the little golden ball then, and they
went running further and further after it?

BOLL: Exactly, always after the gleaming orb, and the orb headed
straight for Parum showing the way in the dark—they are back
in Parum long since, Greta, and still playing with it.

GRETA: But Boll was young and slender and ruddy-complexioned—
and now he's Blue Boll again?

BOLL: What does it matter to you, Greta? Yes, I was young and
slender, as good as . . . Greta, as good as, and that's why you
kissed me in the dark. Don't you remember what the night-
watchman said?

GRETA: I ran with you and you said, 'The children have gone on
ahead'—that's why I ran. I was tired already and got faint and
wanted to run faster and faster—yes, it was dark!

BOLL: Very! But you didn't run for long, and you were soon lying
on the ground and not moving a limb or saying a word—and I
raised you up and carried you with difficulty—[*points to the wall*]—
to the door of this house, opposite the Hotel, and he got his tip
and said 'Thanks' and said I should just let my little bride have a
proper sleep because she certainly needed it, and laughed like these
crafty fellows do. Bride, he said, Greta, for that was the only
explanation that occurred to him.

GRETA: And then I kissed you?

BOLL: In the dark—in the dark I was young and slender, Greta. And
I also understood what you meant when you kept saying: poison,

poison—yes, I could smell it and knew then why you were laughing and weeping and coughing at first but finished up snoring. So I was young and slender—gladly—in the dark.

GRETA: And then?

BOLL: And then I turned my back on the Golden Orb Hotel and fetched the key out of my pocket and opened the tower door, and once in there we naturally ended up in the main building—it wasn't exactly what I wanted, would much rather have taken you somewhere else, but I suppose it had to be. And you lay there and slept, slept deeply and well, and I kept watch up and down, up and down in the dark. Can heaven be more peaceful—think, how peaceful!

GRETA: Do you remember how noisy it was in hell, and how the bare soles were placed on the red-hot coals? Elias knows how to go about things, Blue Boll, and he gave me a lot of poison.

BOLL: Elias? Right you are, Greta, Elias was indeed part of it—now then, Greta, what are you looking at? What is it about little wooden Peter that catches your eye—hmm?

GRETA: *keeps looking from the figure of the apostle to* BOLL *and back again, laughs*] Oh, the way he looks, the way both of you look! The sun is shining into his face and his eyes are as big as saucers; is he hunting for lice or why is he digging about in his big beard?

BOLL: Him? Oh, Him! Look, now the sun is shining into my face too, and a shadowy Boll is growing on the wall, the wooden Saint and my shadow stand face to face, and they clearly show from what kind of flesh they fall. He was once in the flesh too and I still am—just look, Greta.

GRETA: He is closing his mouth and his eyes are flashing.

BOLL: Burning, burning—and mine?

GRETA: Yours—ah, Blue Boll, that's not your best feature. One should really feel ashamed at having to peer out through these heavy shutters you have over your eyes. Apart from that the eyes themselves are alright, but they are hidden in walnut-shells of fat. He has a mouth but he keeps it shut.

BOLL: Tight! It has nothing to say, nothing it wants to say, except for something special from time to time—no more than a half dozen words, done to a turn—and my mouth?

GRETA: Your mouth? Boll, yours is not bad, good at yawning and showing its teeth and at providing plenty of rubbish for the teeth to dispose of. But your teeth are very good, they can cope—as for him, look at him, what hollow cheeks, no room there for teeth, the chamber has thin walls and empty beds. Maybe it's because he has no teeth that his eyes burn as they do and he can look towards things other than flesh.

BOLL: No, he is hungry, Greta—and you must admit hungry is something I don't look!

GRETA: His brow is cleft if you look closely—two lovely, sheer shells!

BOLL: And mine?

GRETA: Blue Boll, you are a good Blue Boll, but I wish I hadn't kissed you. Your cheek is smooth under that hair and your brow is a brow because it's where a brow ought to be. That's about all you could say.

BOLL: You wanted to say something more about Elias, Greta: what was it?

GRETA: It really is like heaven here, we'd better just be quiet—and besides I'm tired. The poison is still scratching at the back of my eyes, like to go home—but there was some reason why I can't—[*presses her hands to her forehead*]—want to leave right away, but I'll sit a bit yet.

BOLL: No need for you to go, Greta. While you were asleep I was across the way and got poor old Saugwurm up. Saugwurm's getting the coach ready, Greta. [*looks at his watch*] You can leave soon and drive to Parum—and Saugwurm'll be back before the ladies and gents get their boots and shoes polished. But tell me what it was like with Elias!

GRETA: You shall hear what you want to hear—you say it, I'll repeat it after you.

BOLL: Look now, Greta, even if the shadow on the wall is not beautiful the almighty sun painted it there honourably and without mocking—will you be angrier with me than the sun? Becoming, you know, Greta, is a hard nut, and when you roll up in Parum you can climb out there as if the owner of the coach were the man in the moon and Boll a scarecrow somewhere else. You can do that, and that is Boll's bitter work and this my becoming has accomplished by the sweat of its brow—but becoming and prospering are to have their due and so Blue Boll will depart his dread vale of tears for the bright country where no dread mystery dwells and hurrah for Boll in the tower! How about that?

GRETA: Finish what you want to say.

BOLL: Ah, yes, Greta, you made the start, with you Boll caught an inkling of what becoming tastes like. Such an ascent shall be his from now on, more and more perfectly.

GRETA: Go on, Blue Boll.

BOLL: Boll has no choice left, Boll must prepare himself for the glory of becoming and that is why he has had the coach harnessed up and Saugwurm will drive the dear witch home at the trot, safe and sound, safe and sound, Greta, you know that now—safe and sound home to her dear children. And Boll will wave his honourable right hand in farewell to what is never to return— and then he applies himself to his removal from the beloved vale of tears and hastens on to enter in safe and sound—but where? The banquet hall of the ineluctable At-Some-Future-Time—you see, Greta, that is how it has to be, the only way it can be.

GRETA: Finish what you have to say, Blue Boll.

BOLL: God, Greta, how much rather I'd stay in the dear vale of tears where I lead such a merry life and may live no longer. Boll's spirit is willing to set forth on its stony path but the flesh is weak. Not a word about Elias!

GRETA: I am quite ready to believe it all—and I'm sure it's true that I was your first trial effort and it must have been pretty hard work! But listen, who on earth was that mighty woman, Elias's devil of a wife, she was the one who pulled me out of his claws, and that's a fact which nobody can deny. Are you pleased to hear that? When the sun shines into your eyes, they burn brighter than his; I see that clearly when I look closely.

BOLL: No wonder—can he do anything with his eyes but let them be seen—but I use my eyes to see with and see you sitting there and hear you speak the truth, and your eyes tell me you are a whole and healthy woman now. [*looks at his watch*] You can leave immediately. I'll take you to the coach—right, off you go!

GRETA [*hesitating*]: And where does that leave you, Blue Boll, if you can't be merry any more?

BOLL: Never mind that, Greta, Boll can't help giving birth to Boll, you'll see, Boll's birth and tower-high transformation are at the door. Everybody is his own best neighbour and when it comes to one's own development one has to know how to go about it. *The tower door can be heard creaking, they look round.*

BOLL: This is a stroke of luck, Martha, we can breakfast together right away—no, no, come closer, you're not disturbing us in the least.

MRS. BOLL *comes.*

MRS. BOLL: But will it be alright with her?

BOLL: Kiss my lady's hand, Greta, this is Boll's wife—come along, no need to be so timid—come along, won't you?

MRS. BOLL: *waves her off*] I just happened to look out of my window . . . you were crossing the square and disappeared into the church . . .

BOLL: Kiss her hand, Greta! [GRETA *does so with extreme repugnance, clumsily and fearfully,* MRS. BOLL *hardly lets her do it*] She's going away and never coming back, Martha, never again, the Greta she was; Saugwurm is probably waiting outside the 'Golden Orb' as you will have noticed, I hope—yes, never again, never again.

MRS. BOLL: Wouldn't it be better if you said nothing at all to me about all this Kurt? No, I really can't understand our dear Lord any more. [*turns away and puts a hand on her forehead*] Not the slightest chance of a wink of sleep the way this night has gone— and don't I always get migraine after this kind of business? [*back again*] God, Kurt—you've probably still not heard anything about what happened tonight?

BOLL: I think I have—plenty, more than enough, but perhaps something else has happened?

MRS. BOLL: So you really don't know yet? I should never have believed it!

BOLL: What was it then, Martha, if you don't mind?

MRS. BOLL: How could you know—who could . . . [*to* GRETA] I have to inform my husband, who is unfortunately completely unprepared, of a shattering occurrence in the family.

GRETA: Yes, Mrs. Boll.

MRS. BOLL: She does not understand, Kurt.

BOLL: *to* GRETA] If you want to do something more for me, Greta, you can go up to the altar and say an 'Our Father' for me. As if I were someone who does not have the time or can't find the courage to do it for himself—will you, Greta?

GRETA *turns,* BOLL *accompanies her several paces and shows her the way to the altar.* GRETA *off.*

BOLL: So you slept badly, Martha, and migraine too, as always after this kind of business?

MRS. BOLL: It's just one thing after another, Kurt.

BOLL: Excitements of this kind, Martha, if you will permit me, are a good excuse to take a sleeping tablet—but I interrupted you.

MRS. BOLL: Are you capable of listening, Kurt? If you get in the least bit dizzy, or even . . .

BOLL: Doesn't matter, I'm to be the first to hear your tale, I suppose, so go ahead!

MRS. BOLL: You'd better sit down there, Kurt, and make up your mind right from the start to take care not to let yourself get worked up about this—my God, time will heal anyway and you will say what happened could have happened long since—or maybe not till later—I should really never have believed it!

BOLL: Alright, Martha—now I am really ready for anything—if you will be so good.

MRS. BOLL: You maybe remember that you and Otto did not exactly part as friends last night?

BOLL: Otto and I? That kind of thing has happened plenty times before—all forgotten already—did he say anything else?

MRS. BOLL: Oh, Kurt, how can I break it to you gently and considerately enough? First he kept on drinking all on his own, said he had to burn that Lord God out of his system with pure spirits—and then when he wanted to go to bed, Bertha had just gone to sleep and he disturbed her into the bargain, and then he collapsed full length in front of the wash-stand. It was as well the man they call Lord happened to be so handy, in fact he was sleeping right next door and Bertha only had to knock. People like that are really quite good to have around on such occasions. We did all the necessary—now he is lying quietly in bed and the man is sitting beside him and speaking to him. But he is really remarkably changed, Kurt, and his hand shakes all the time. He can't speak. The doctor thinks he'll probably make a fairly complete recovery this time—I should never have believed it.

BOLL: You are quite right with your wise words—that could have happened to him long since, or again he might well have reached that stage some time soon or later maybe—you see how composed I am?

MRS. BOLL: Yes, Kurt, that's good, but I really am terribly sorry—poor Otto!

BOLL: Is he dead perhaps—is this to be broken to me gradually—as far as I am concerned, you see, he could just as well be dead. Living accommodation in the vale of tears which has changed so much can at best be only a pig-sty now.

MRS. BOLL: How can you say such things, Kurt; no, thanks and praise be to God—he is still alive.

BOLL: But much changed, and his hand shakes? Well, well, who would have thought that of Otto; no, I too should never have believed it! I'm ready to wager this way of becoming was easier for him than the hard trial run I had with Greta was for me. That Otto—now he speaks as with the tongues of angels, there's a roaring in my ears, I can tell you, just as if one of the old dames had put her trumpet to his lips and he were blowing it with all his might. [shouts] Do you hear, Greta?

GRETA: [from within] Yes, Mr. Boll?

BOLL: Suppose you've finished the prayer, if you haven't spent too much time thinking about the first part of it. It's not a question of courage with me any more. [to MRS. BOLL] Remarkable, how easy talking with this witch gets; have you any explanation for it?

GRETA: [from behind] Boll, I hear her again.

BOLL: I can't, Greta.

GRETA: [behind] I can hear that devil woman again. I have pleaded and wept, but she said, 'He must be his own judge'—but from me you shall have forgiveness.

BOLL: That's it, is it, now I know. [GRETA comes back. MRS. BOLL about to speak].

BOLL: Quite right, Martha, that's how it is, exactly.

MRS. BOLL: But I didn't say anything!

BOLL: What difference does that make, you are always in the right, I knew that beforehand—but I should not have cut you off like that—don't be angry, do you hear? [he puts his arm round her, at the same time taking GRETA by the arm and walking a few steps with both of them along the aisle, up and down, and then he stops in front of the apostle] Look at that surly old fellow, children—earlier, I felt I was becoming afraid of his wooden Grandezza, but now I stand before him with uncommon indifference. I can bare my teeth at you, you with your mug full of silence, and can ridicule you, say what you will, you sullen piece of toothlessness. Is he saying anything, Martha, do you hear anything, Greta? What I have had in life I have cherished, cherished, as it was given to me, and what has become of it—all the same, this was a must for Boll, a must, a must . . . Children, he is shaking his head. Can you see it, Martha, no truly, he knows better. Alright, just look at him once more: arid through and through but nothing wasted, you can tell just from his manner why he had to become so, for him too there was a must, a must. What do you say, Martha?

MRS. BOLL: Do you want me to die of shame? I'll faint if you don't let me out of this hell. I'll scream Kurt.

BOLL: Don't scream, Martha, and do more than that: be good to her—and don't talk about feeling ashamed!

MRS. BOLL: I must scream, I shall scream.

BOLL: Martha, remember how much we owe to her—you must, you must remember that, and that's why you must kiss her hand, that is what you must do for her. She forgives for her part, and you must honour her for your part: kiss her hand and then see that she gets to the coach safely. That's the way I want things to be. [MRS. BOLL *speaks incomprehensible words through her tears*].

BOLL: And yet, and yet, you are right at that! Some warming influence is at work from heaven on high. Class, you say? Property owner's wife, you say? And so on, and so on? I tell you, you are Boll's wife, and Boll's class has an upper and a lower end. We are at the lower end. The honey of humility can help you out of your sour static state towards sweet becoming—give yourself a shake, wake up! [*shakes her*].

MRS. BOLL, *pushed by* BOLL *towards* GRETA, *takes her hand and bends over it.* GENTLEMAN *enters from the back.*

BOLL: *without looking round*] How is Otto?

GENTLEMAN: Well, well as never before, Mr. Boll. Your cousin followed without difficulty the second, slight little sign from a gentle hand—it came with the most deliberate ease, just as an easily grasped allusion conjures up a ready smile . . .

BOLL: That's it, that's how it is! Everything is going black. [*frees himself, pushes the women out gently*] Do it, round things off properly; Martha, lead her to the coach and help her—it is for me, and what you do for me you do for yourself.

MRS. BOLL *and* GRETA *off.*

BOLL: *to* GENTLEMAN] So all that was needed was a slight little sign and Otto's trembling right hand became steady again? Changes are coming thick and fast, aren't they—I can even feel quite a considerable something stirring within myself, with Otto becoming has completely gone to seed. So I thank you for all the attention . . . thanks, but I don't need any further assistance. [*waves impatiently towards the door*].

GENTLEMAN: After you, Mr. Boll! [*they look at each other*, BOLL *conceals his confusion with difficulty*].

GENTLEMAN: And how are things with you? Perhaps it was only the brilliance of your masterly description of a fall last evening, which now leads me to enquire . . .

BOLL: Oh, rubbish, who ever worries about things like that, on the morning after!

GENTLEMAN: And yet—what is there left when you think it over carefully? What is there left for you to do? And if you hesitate, nothing at all will come of it, I can tell you that now—it's all over in two or three minutes.

BOLL: Two or three—but listen, what minutes they will be!

GENTLEMAN: The more words, the more delay, the more torment. Mr. Boll, you've hardly got the breath to struggle up high enough. I can hear the whistling in your chest. Your breathing is laboured: in—out. And it has to take you at least as far as the first window. How did it go last night—a little zephyr descends, and the pavement red with Boll's blood?

BOLL: *sits down*] Quite right, that's what was to happen, that's what I foresaw—my breath . . .

GENTLEMAN: You had the breath to produce a brilliant description of your fall—as for the fall itself . . .

BOLL: We—shall—come to some arrangement, my breath and I. I thank you and that is that—the door *is* open, isn't it?

GENTLEMAN: I'd rather leave after you. I have plenty of time and should like to help your plans along as much as possible. Don't wait; with every second of delay it becomes more difficult.

BOLL: *bounds up*] Lord, what an absolute devil you are, what a nerve you have.

GENTLEMAN: So you've got your strength back, I see, seize the fresh moment, don't give a thought to the void I'm showing you, Mr Boll, Mr. Boll!

BOLL: *up to him, gasping for breath*] I have enough, there's still enough. You'll see what for. [*shakes him*].

GENTLEMAN: Fine, that's me punished, there was enough for that, but I'm afraid it cost you your last ounce of strength. Will you still be capable of accomplishing it?

BOLL: *leans for support, collects himself*] Let's again give a thought to the rules of politeness, let us vie with each other in civilities—so—after you! [*gestures towards the door*].

GENTLEMAN: The time is up—too late, Mr. Boll, there is a time for everything. Becoming, you know, that down-off-the-tower, primitive kind of becoming is past. Is it reasonable to make a fresh start by putting an end to it all?

BOLL: But how could you have the nerve, how could you bring yourself to coerce me in such an unheard-of fashion?

GENTLEMAN: Ssh! I risked it trusting to the other Boll, the one who stands above the old Boll and strives out beyond him to the new beginning, who rejects and forbids ending. You know what I mean, and that I am right when I say: Boll has wrestled with Boll, Boll has judged Boll, and he, the other, the new Boll, has triumphed.

BOLL: Boll, you claim, has judged Boll—and do you think I could still live on?

GENTLEMAN: Live on? Certainly not, but anew—yes! It has been proven—you must, Boll must give birth to the new Boll, and what a one he will be—there are better prospects for the future than the plunge from the church tower can offer. Good prospects —for there is substance and striving in you; suffering and struggling, dear sir, are the organs of becoming—Already your breath is calm and regular and will serve, I promise you, for a fruitful struggle and will have strength to support you. Boll becomes through Boll—and becoming, sir, becoming is fulfilled out of time, and duration is only blind appearance. This I submit for your good judgement, and whatsoever is more cometh of evil. [*off*].

BOLL: *falls on his knees, flailing around him with his arms, then slowly he raises his head and looks up to the apostle*] Did you say that? Kept your mouth closed for so long, to make ready the word? Boll must? Must? Well then—*I will.*